# The Blind Visionary

**Practical Lessons for Meeting Challenges on the Way to a More Fulfilling Life and Career**

**Doug Eadie and Virginia Jacko**

With a Foreword by José Feliciano

A Governance Edge Publication

A Governance Edge® Publication
3 Sunny Point Terrace
Oldsmar, FL 34677

(800) 209-7652
Email: info@GovernanceEdge.com

A complete list of books and CDs from Governance Edge is available
at www.GovernanceEdge.com.

ISBN 978-0-9798894-4-8

Library of Congress Control Number: 2009943013

Library of Congress Subject Headings:
Success in business
Leadership
Women executives
Blind women—Biography
Retinitis pigmentosa

Book & cover design by Darlene & Dan Swanson of
Van-garde Imagery, Inc. • www.van-garde.com
Cover image by Cristian Lazzari • www.cristianlazzari.com

To the Board of Directors, staff, clients, and supporters of the Miami Lighthouse for the Blind and Visually Impaired

# Contents

# Foreword

Virginia Jacko's amazing odyssey has all the makings of a great read, and as one of only a handful of blind chief executives in the United States, her story is an inspiration to everyone who hears it.

I have come to value Virginia not only as a colleague in working on behalf of the blind and visually impaired, but also as a friend. As you learn about Virginia's personal and professional journey in her own words, you'll come to know why so many do, indeed, call her "friend."

They say that truth can be stranger than fiction; and here in this case, it would be difficult to make up a story that so vividly demonstrates triumph in attitude, courage, creativity, and tenacity over adversity. But that truly has been the case here: Virginia's story is about mustering the courage to take action—to embrace change in the face of a devastating blow (losing her eyesight in the midst of a successful career in higher education). She could have easily been overwhelmed—retreating to her home, disengaging from the world and bemoaning her fate, but she did the very opposite!

Virginia has a powerful calling that motivates her fundamental purpose in life—that is, *to contribute* and *to make a difference.* This calling has driven her to ultimately start over again from the bottom, professionally speaking, seeking vocational rehabilitation training at the Miami Lighthouse for the Blind and Visually Impaired where she now helps others along their own path, with their own personal odyssey, toward independence and success. I love a happy ending!

José Feliciano
Weston, CT
November 2009

# Acknowledgments

We, alone, could not have written this book, nor can we take sole credit for whatever virtues it might have. No book is the product solely of its authors, and although there are too many for us to acknowledge them by name, we want to thank the teachers and colleagues who, over the past forty years, by their words and by their examples, have shaped our thinking. They are, in a very real sense, our coauthors.

We owe a significant debt to the Miami Lighthouse for the Blind and Visually Impaired. Through the Miami Lighthouse, Virginia not only acquired indispensable personal and professional skills, but also discovered a new, more passionate calling in life and a rewarding career that enables her to translate this calling into action day after day. And the Miami Lighthouse, through its High-Impact Governing Initiative, made it possible for Doug to meet and get to know Virginia, first as a colleague and eventually as a friend and coauthor. Virginia, as president and CEO of the Lighthouse, has arranged for her royalties from this book to be paid directly to the Lighthouse—to help this important institution continue its wonderful work of transforming lives and unleashing human potential.

We greatly appreciate the wise counsel and very capable assistance of William Eadie, president of Governance Edge, LLC, the publisher, who offered insightful advice and shepherded our book through the publication process, and of Thomas Berger, whose sensitive editing certainly made this a better book than it otherwise would have been.

Our book has benefited from the comments of a number of reviewers, including: Angela Ashe; Steve Bland; Tracey Burns; Jennifer Eadie; MaryEllen Elia; Jeff Finkle; Jane Gallucci; Robert Jacko; Justin King; Barbara Krai; John McConnell; Jim McGuirk; Steve Marcus; Kay Sue Nagle; Cathy Ordiway; Shan Shikarpuri; and William Werther.

And, finally, without the love, steadfast support, and insightful counsel of Doug's wife, Barbara Krai, and Virginia's husband, Bob Jacko, this would not only be a lesser book, it most likely would not even exist.

Doug Eadie and Virginia Jacko

Oldsmar and Miami, Florida

November 2009

# PREFACE

## THE WHY AND WHAT OF THIS BOOK

### WHY READ THIS BOOK?

We are confident you will find this account of Virginia's Purdue and Miami Lighthouse years captivating and perhaps even inspirational, but in writing this book we have aimed higher than merely telling a fascinating true story. If you aspire to live richer, more fulfilling and satisfying personal and professional lives, we have written this book for you. Our goal is to provide you with very practical guidance that you can put to immediate use in your life, drawing on Virginia's odyssey at Purdue University, where she began to lose her eyesight, and at the Miami Lighthouse for the Blind and Visually Impaired, where Virginia began as a vocational rehabilitation student and is now the blind CEO. Here is what we hope for you: that—armed with the lessons that we draw from Virginia's experience—you will come to a fuller understanding of your life's mission—your fundamental calling; that, guided by your calling, you will take advantage of opportunities to take action, no matter how circumscribed your situation might be or how daunting the challenges you face at any particular time; and that, as a consequence of acting, you create a life that is infused with richer meaning and greater satisfaction.

Throughout the writing of this book, we have been keenly aware that you, the reader, and every other human being are unique in many ways—cognitive ability; personality; character; personal history; current circumstances; social and cultural affinities, and more. We are individuals, not generalizations, and we know that Virginia's unique story cannot, in its rich detail, be yours. For example, her education and her experience as a sighted executive at Purdue without question laid a foundation for her eventual success as the blind president and CEO of the Miami Lighthouse for the Blind and Visually Impaired. And her success, both at Purdue and the Lighthouse, also owes much to her inherent optimism, her can-do spirit, her affinity for finance, and her facility with numbers. Not everyone aspires to, or can even become, a nonprofit chief executive, whether sighted or blind. Aspirations, goals, abilities, and circumstances are unique to the individual. That said, we are confident that Virginia's odyssey at Purdue and the Lighthouse is the stuff of valuable lessons worth sharing with you and other readers.

## THE STRUCTURE OF OUR BOOK

The book that you are reading really got started on December 19, 2008, when we met for a full day at Virginia's spacious condo in Grove Isle south of downtown Miami, with a beautiful view of Biscayne Bay. Our primary objective was for Virginia to tell Doug the story of her Purdue and Miami Lighthouse years in as much detail as the time allowed. A digital recorder sat on the table between us, and Virginia's new guide dog, Gibney, lay at her feet. Fortunately, Virginia's husband, Bob, a professor of engineering at Purdue, was in Miami for the holidays, so that evening over dinner he could help flesh out the canvas of Virginia's life and career.

Any doubts we might have had about coauthoring this book evaporated over the course of this highly productive and thoroughly enjoyable daylong session, and we both ended the day enthusiastic about the writing enterprise. In addition to generating considerable content we could use in the book we had set out to write, we also came up with this book's somewhat unconventional structure: After our Preface, Parts One and Two would recount Virginia's years at Purdue and the Miami Lighthouse in her own words, drawing on many more hours spent together with the recorder. In Part Three, we would engage in a dialogue, discussing the major lessons to be drawn from Virginia's odyssey that would help our readers in their own journeys. The book would conclude with three postscripts: Doug telling his story of meeting and working with Virginia at the Miami Lighthouse; a discussion of authors who especially influenced our thinking and writing; and a brief history of the Miami Lighthouse. Our writing mission was now crystal clear, and we never looked back from that point on.

## THE MIRACLE OF SERENDIPITY

We feel blessed that we were presented with, and that we acted on, the opportunity to write this book together. It could easily not have happened—if we had not met and worked together as consultant and client, if we had not shared a passionate interest in human change and growth, if Doug had not already set substantial time aside to write another book that was preempted by this joint effort, and, of course, if we had not recognized the wonderful educational potential in Vir-

ginia's odyssey. In *The Road Less Traveled*, the physician M. Scott Peck
writes about the "miracle of serendipity." Seeing serendipity, which
Webster defines as "the gift of finding valuable or agreeable things not
sought for," as a form of grace, Peck writes that "one of the reasons
we fail to take full advantage of grace is that we are not fully aware
of its presence—that is, we don't find valuable things not sought for,
because we fail to appreciate the value of the gift when it is given us."
We are certainly grateful for the miracle of serendipity that led to this
creative collaboration, which is much more than just the product of
foresightedness and sound planning. We see our writing partnership
as a concrete manifestation of grace at work in our lives, and we are
thankful for the gift.

## THE MATTER OF BLINDNESS

There is the matter of Virginia's blindness, which we have spent many
hours discussing as this book has taken shape. To be sure, blindness
is the defining challenge in Virginia's personal life and her career. Her
overcoming blindness in the sense of continuing to function effec-
tively at Purdue as a senior financial executive and eventually finding
a new mission in her life, becoming a highly successful and fulfilled
chief executive who happens to be blind, is the primary story this
book tells and the source of the lessons we share in Part Three of this
book. But we strongly believe that Virginia's blindness, per se, should
not be the focus of this book, either in terms of the detailed nature of
this particular challenge or of the specific strategies and technologies
for overcoming this specific disability.

Blindness in this book is a symbol, albeit a dramatic one, for any
challenge that might limit your life, narrowing your vision and con-

straining your sphere of action—from the purely psychological, such as extreme performance anxiety, to the purely physical, such as losing your eyesight. And Virginia's struggle to overcome her particular challenge—blindness—her quest to live a full and fulfilling life of tremendous accomplishment in the face of this particular challenge—should be seen as representative of any effort to take action in the face of adversity, to resist becoming a passive victim, to fight the potential narrowing of freedom in your life. So this book is for everyone, everywhere, who aspires to live life as fully as possible in the face of whatever challenges come their way, fulfilling their promise and carrying out the mission that is uniquely theirs.

## ON TO VIRGINIA'S STORY

Now we turn to Virginia's years at Purdue University, where she managed for several years to carry out her demanding responsibilities as a senior financial executive in the face of her failing eyesight, and ultimately set a dramatic new course for herself at the Miami Lighthouse for the Blind.

# PART ONE

## PURDUE: THE GROWING DARKNESS

### DOUG'S OVERVIEW

December 20, 2000, was Virginia Jacko's last day at Purdue University. It turned out that her career at Purdue was over, although she did not know it at the time. Rapidly losing her eyesight due to a condition known as retinitis pigmentosa, Virginia had taken a three-month leave of absence to enroll herself in the Miami Lighthouse for the Blind and Visually Impaired. Virginia had not submitted her resignation to the University. After completing her vocational rehabilitation training at the Lighthouse, she fully intended to return to Purdue, where she was a solidly established, highly successful financial executive who found tremendous satisfaction in her work.

Virginia's rise through the ranks in the Business Office at Purdue had been exceptional. Beginning in 1978 as a part-time business manager assigned to the School (now College) of Liberal Arts, within four years Virginia was the full-time chief financial manager for the vice president of student services, which involved financial oversight of fifteen departments and other departmental business managers. By

1985, Virginia was serving as special assistant to the vice president for business services, and within five years, began working directly with the University president and provost as their business manager. Who knows where her career in higher education finance would have taken her had not her rapidly advancing blindness led to this dramatic turning point in her life and career? But Virginia being Virginia, she dealt with her failing eyesight by taking aggressive action, setting off on a new path—with no clear destination in mind—and never looking back.

Virginia had arrived in West Lafayette, Indiana, in 1969 with her husband, Bob, who joined the Purdue faculty after earning his doctorate in engineering there. Virginia, although earning her master's degree at Purdue while Bob worked on his doctorate, had been out of the workforce for seven years—much of that time as a stay-at-home mother raising their three children—when she applied for Purdue's only part-time business manager position in 1978. Going for the job was an easy decision to make. With the kids now in school, she had time and energy to spare, as her life at home alone now revolved around tennis dates and driving to the kids' sporting events, leaving her feeling increasingly unfulfilled. Virginia was also obviously well qualified for the business manager position, which involved handling the financial affairs of several departments and institutes in Purdue's School of Liberal Arts. She had worked as a financial analyst at banks in Chicago and Milwaukee and in the accounting department of a manufacturing firm in Cedar Rapids before putting her career on hold to tackle the challenge of full-time motherhood.

Although she loved being a full-time mother, Virginia knew that the time had come to rejoin the workforce. For one thing, she recognized that if she was going to be truly happy and deeply satisfied, she had to have the stimulation of a challenging job that capitalized on her talent and experience. For another, she knew that if she stayed out of the workforce much longer, she might very well seriously jeopardize her professional advancement. So back to work Virginia went, and she recognized early-on that she had made the right decision. She loved everything about the job—getting the budget out; reviewing and signing off on requisitions; monitoring expenditures; the whole ball of wax—and she was very, very good at what she did. So good, in fact, that it was not long before her boss in the Liberal Arts business office asked her to expand her work to three-quarter-time and to add new departments to her business manager portfolio. Instead, Virginia decided that it made sense to apply for a full-time position, and she was appointed business manager of the largest department in Liberal Arts, which turned out to be the launching pad for Virginia's rapid rise as a financial executive at Purdue.

Virginia's new business manager responsibility was a major step up: a department with large federal research grants from the Departments of Defense and Education, the National Institutes of Health, and the National Science Foundation; a budget of around $10 million; and more than one hundred employees. Her next job—special assistant to the vice president for student services, whose domain included fifteen administrative departments, such as admissions, financial aid, the dean of students, the student hospital, and Purdue's musical organizations—took her even farther up the Purdue administrative ladder. Now that she was located in Hovde Hall, known as the "head shed," which housed Purdue's top executive echelon, including the president, provost, and treasurer (head of the business office hierarchy), Virginia's responsibilities expanded rapidly over the next few years. It was not long before Virginia was working directly with Purdue's president, provost, treasurer, Board of Trustees secretary, and a number of vice presidents. By this time, she was also the only Purdue administrator authorized to sign documents for the president and provost, such as faculty appointments, sabbatical approvals, and conflict of interest disclosures.

Life was good for Virginia at Purdue University. Her husband, Bob, was a highly respected tenured professor of civil engineering. Their daughter Julie was doing graduate work at Purdue, on her way to becoming the first child of a Purdue engineering professor to be awarded a Purdue engineering PhD. Their second daughter, Suellyn, was doing graduate work in pharmacy toward her Doctor of Pharmacy degree, and their son, Robert, was a Purdue undergraduate. Virginia loved her expanding role at Hovde Hall, relishing the increasingly complex executive challenges she was grappling with. As her responsibilities had grown, and as she had successfully dealt with one complex financial and administrative issue after another, her vision of what she was capable of achieving professionally had expanded accordingly. Virginia's colleagues saw a bright future ahead for her, but she and only a select few knew that fate had dealt her a tremendous blow, forcing her to cope with the challenge of her lifetime: slowly but surely going blind.

In the early 1990s, Virginia had begun to notice problems with her peripheral vision in certain situations, but she did not take these incidents seriously for quite some time and certainly never imagined that she was gradually losing her eyesight, beginning with her peripheral vision. For example, Virginia and Bob enjoyed bird-watching, which was becoming increasingly difficult, and there were problems on the tennis court. Virginia had always held her own in doubles at the Purdue Women's Club, but the ball began to go in and out of her field of vision, which she at first attributed to lapses in concentration. As her vision-related problems steadily grew worse, Virginia and Bob, deciding that she needed to be checked out, went to a nationally respected medical center, where she was informed that she was probably in the early stages of multiple sclerosis. A second prestigious medical center that Virginia and Bob consulted determined, based on a spinal tap, that she did not have multiple sclerosis and diagnosed optic atrophy in only one eye. This was reassuring news, relatively speaking.

But things were clearly getting worse. A defining moment occurred in 1995, when Virginia quit driving after hitting and dragging three wooden horses surrounding a construction site through an intersection. She had never seen them. In 1998, she learned the truth about her condition. Still believing that she was suffering from optic atrophy in one eye, she went to a low vision doctor to get a loop that she could attach to her glasses so she and Bob could go bird-watching. Imagine her shock when the doctor informed her that she was legally blind since she had no peripheral vision. Alarmed, Virginia and Bob went to a third major medical institution, where she was diagnosed as having retinitis pigmentosa. The disease that eventually led to Virginia's total blindness is a group of disorders characterized by progressive peripheral vision loss and night-vision difficulties that can—and did in Virginia's case—lead to central vision loss. Retinitis pigmentosa is commonly thought of as a rod-cone dystrophy in which the genetic defects cause cell death, predominantly in the rod photoreceptors, which are primarily responsible for light perception and peripheral vision. The cone photoreceptors, which handle color perception, die in a similar manner early or late in the various forms of the disease. It is estimated that the incidence of retinitis pigmentosa in the United States is one in four thousand.

## Doug and Virginia in Conversation

### Doug:

Before we talk about the onset of retinitis pigmentosa and how you were able to keep functioning at such a high level as a financial executive at Purdue, would you say a bit more about your rapid rise through the University's administrative hierarchy?

### Virginia:

Let me start at the beginning by telling you about a turning point that got my career at Purdue University really going. You know that I rejoined the workforce in 1978 as a part-time business manager at Purdue. That job went so well my boss came to me with a proposition. "You know, Virginia," he said, "I'm aware you prefer to be home when your kids arrive from school at three o'clock, but you're doing so well we'd like to give you a three-quarter-time job that will involve taking on some more departments." And I said, "Well, I'm interested, but isn't the business manager for psychology a full-time position?" By the way, that full-time job had just opened up, but that wasn't what I was being offered. He said, "That's right, but you can handle the departments and institutes we're talking about working three-quarter time and be able to be home for the kids. You'll have some office support." I said, "Well, but I still won't get benefits, right?" He said, "That's right because you've got to be full time." So I called my mother to discuss the offer. When I explained that I'd been offered a new three-quarter-time position so I could be home when the kids got back from school, but that the full-time business manager position for the psychology department was open, she was really adamant about my going for that job. She said, "Someday you're going to retire, and you're going to wish you had benefits. If I were you, I'd forget about the part-time job and just apply for the full-time position in psychology." And, with Mother's encouragement, I went for it.

That was a really significant moment in my life because I said, "But, Mom, I'm going to have to get a babysitter for the kids." She said, "That's okay. You kids all grew up with babysitters. Forget this part-time stuff and having to be home with the kids. Go for a real job and get benefits." So I said to my boss, "I'd really like to have a full-time job." He said, "We were hoping that you would take on the additional work on a part-time basis." I said, "I just think that if the previous person had it as a full-time job, it must be a full-time job." Well, the upshot was, he agreed, and I took on the full-time job. And guess what: The person that they hired to do what I'd previously been doing, that also became a full-time job. Now I was really on my way up the ladder.

You've already talked about how I ended up at Hovde Hall, working directly with the president, provost, and treasurer, along with several of the vice presidents, so I'm not going to go over that. Let me just say a few words about my approach to every job I had at Purdue and tell you a couple of stories that will help explain why my duties had expanded so dramatically by the time I began really struggling with my deteriorating eyesight. Above all else, Doug, I always thought of the officers I did financial analysis and other administrative work for as my customers, and the customer was almost always right. They deserved to get the "products" they asked for as long as they were reasonable and feasible, and I always went really out of my way to pitch in and help get the job done, even if it wasn't my responsibility. For example, one day the provost called me in to discuss the annual budget preparation process. He wanted a frequency distribution of faculty raises and asked me to get to the budget office about this. When I conveyed the request to the fellow in the budget office, he said, "Virginia, we've never done that." I said, "I know, but I'll help you. That's what we're going to do." And at first they hated it because it wasn't their thing, but I really insisted: "But this is what he wants. We've got to do it, and if we don't, he'll just find someone else."

And when my preeminent customers—the president, provost, and treasurer—wanted something that the person directly responsible wouldn't do, then I'd just go ahead and do it myself, rather than disappoint my customers. For example, the budget office invariably crunched numbers and put together a humongous binder for the president's management review meetings and, as far as they were concerned, that was that; they'd done their job and weren't about to budge. But I'd been a financial analyst for years, and I have a very good analytical mind, so I could go through that stuff, and I could give my customers a two-page summary of the most important points. When a fellow from the budget office protested that it wasn't their job to do that kind of thing, I simply said: "They asked for it, you guys were dragging your feet, so I went ahead and did the job. End of story." Don't get me wrong; I was happy for the budget people to put a summary together, but when they resisted, I didn't really have a choice. The customer always came first to me.

My can-do approach is probably the most important reason for my success in various roles at Purdue. "No" and "can't" were my least favorite words at Purdue, and they still are! So it was kind of inevitable that new functions kept coming my way, like being put in charge of developing the agenda and materials for the president's management review meetings and eventually even reviewing and signing key documents for both the president and provost.

## DOUG:

It must have been a crushing blow, being diagnosed with retinitis pigmentosa after coming so far at Purdue and performing so well at a series of jobs you really loved.

## VIRGINIA:

Well, the thing is, Doug, losing my sight wasn't like being hit with a bolt of lightning. Remember, it was a very gradual process that began well before I was diagnosed with retinitis pigmentosa in 1998, and there were a couple of incorrect diagnoses along the way: first multiple sclerosis and then optic atrophy in only one of my eyes. Bob and I eventually realized that something really serious was going on and got the right diagnosis, but it happened very slowly. In that kind of situation, you make adjustments, at least I did, and you don't necessarily assume the worst. Actually, in my and my husband Bob's memory, the most emotional time was when we were told I had multiple sclerosis. That evening, we were like, "Wow, this is really terrible," and we did have a bit too much wine. But I told Bob, "I don't believe it. I feel too good. So let's wait and see what happens." You know, that night was more of a smack in the face than the blindness because the blindness moved so slowly—was really insidious.

Actually, I'm not even sure when my sight began to go downhill, it was so gradual, and, anyway, I didn't have any reason to believe, until 1998, that I had a serious eye condition. There were signs, sure, but they weren't dramatic, or especially worrisome, and, anyway, I was charging ahead with my work and it's not my nature to let minor things throw me off stride. What I remember first is that I began to have trouble driving at night. With retinitis pigmentosa, you start to lose your night vision. I began to look for car lights in front of me and follow them when I drove at night. Early on one night, I remember, I was driving back from a Girl Scouts meeting (I was vice president of the Sycamore Council). That was way out in the country in Indiana, and it was dark, really dark out there. I had to get back home, and I literally waited for a car to pull out in front of me so I could follow that car because I couldn't differentiate between the road and the gravel. But alarm bells didn't go off. I merely thought, "I'm just having trouble seeing at night," that kind of thing. You don't believe—if you don't have a history of blindness in your family—that you've got a real serious problem, at least I didn't for quite some time.

But there were other signs. For example, I played tennis in the Purdue Women's Club league—doubles. When I look back, I remember my partner saying, "You know, Virginia, you'd be such a good tennis player if you would only concentrate." And I'd think to myself, "I really am a good concentrator, so what's my problem?" Like if I was going to serve, I'd say, "Concentrate, Virginia. Keep your eye on the ball, keep your eye on the ball." And for a split second, I'd lose track of the ball. I didn't know it at the time, but the ball was actually leaving my field of vision, but I thought it was a concentration problem. There wasn't any reason to suspect it was my eyes. You know, with retinitis pigmentosa, you lose your eyesight from the outside in. Unlike people with macular degeneration, they lose their central vision first, and you read with your central vision. So those people immediately suspect something serious is going on because they they're having trouble reading. In my case I was losing it out there, so it wasn't that noticeable, for a long time anyway.

Around 1994, I began to get more worried, because there were other signs. Bob and I had always enjoyed bird-watching, for example, and I was beginning to have trouble seeing the birds. That's about the time we decided we needed to get really expert medical advice and were told I probably had multiple sclerosis. And the incident when I hit those wooden horses around a construction site and dragged them through the intersection—that was in 1995, I think—really did get us to thinking. I'd never even seen them, and I thought to myself, "Oh my God, I didn't see them; they could've been students!" I was on my way to the beauty salon, so when I got there I called the kids (my son, Robert, was an undergraduate at Purdue then, and my daughter Julie was doing something on campus) and had them pick me up. I never drove again, that was a real turning point. But Bob and I still didn't know I was going blind. Remember, about that time we got a second opinion, which was that I had optic atrophy in just one of my eyes. It was only when Bob and I went to a low vision doctor in 1998 so I could have my glasses fitted with a loop for bird-watching, that we knew I was really in trouble. So we're in the doctor's office, and he's putting the loop in different places, and I can't see through it. That's when he told me, "Do you know that you're legally blind?" And I said, "No I'm not." And he said, "I just did a field of vision, and you're 20/20 centrally, but when I put this loop over on the side here, you can't see through it because you don't have any vision there. That's a definition of legally blind."

Well that didn't make sense to me. I told him, "Come on now, I just read your eye chart, and I read it all the way down to 20/40." "But what did you do?" he said. "You told me to shut off the lights and show you one letter at a time. So you adapt real quickly, and when I show you one letter at a time you can read all the way down to 20/40. But if I turn the light on and there's not as much contrast, and I ask you to read the entire line, you can't do that because some of those letters are outside of your field of vision." That's when Bob and I really did begin to realize that things were much worse than we'd suspected, and we went off to a really prestigious research hospital and found out I had retinitis pigmentosa and would eventually become completely blind.

**DOUG:**

So, Virginia, you'd been dealing with peripheral vision problems since the early 1990s, you quit driving in 1995, in 1998 you were diagnosed with retinitis pigmentosa, and you knew then that you were inexorably going blind. But you kept working at Purdue until December 2000, when you decided to take medical leave and enroll yourself at the Miami Lighthouse for the Blind. Two questions: Did you ever seriously think about resigning from Purdue, maybe just retiring, before you decided to go on medical leave in November 2000? And how in heaven's name were you able to keep doing your job as your eyesight got increasingly worse?

**VIRGINIA:**

You might not believe this, Doug, but I never once considered resigning from Purdue until the very end, after I'd finished my vocational rehabilitation program at the Lighthouse in the spring of 2001; I never even got seriously depressed during this whole period from the early 1990s until my resignation. Bob and I were talking about this the other day, after you and I had our first interview session, and he'll tell you that he can count on one hand the number of times I cried during this period. And the few times I broke into tears, it wasn't about the cruel blow that fate had dealt me—you know, that kind of thing. It was always over little frustrating incidents. I'm a full-steam-ahead kind of person, and I hate being slowed down, so I get frustrated when things don't go the way I want. But that didn't have anything to do with the big picture. I've never been the kind of person that dwells on problems; I've never sat around saying, "Woe is me, why did this happen to me?" You've got a problem, figure out how to deal with it and get cracking—that was my modus operandi before I started going blind, and it didn't change with retinitis pigmentosa! Over the years I've seen plenty of people turn bumps in the road into mountains that stopped them cold, but life is filled with bumps, there's never going to be a bump-free journey. To me, losing my sight was a pretty big bump, but still just a bump.

Honestly, I never for a moment—after I was diagnosed with retinitis pigmentosa, or before that when all I knew was that I was having increasing difficulties with peripheral vision—thought about throwing in the towel. You see, I was on a professional mission. I haven't told many people this, but I could see myself becoming a university treasurer by the time I got to Hovde Hall, maybe not at Purdue, but at a major institution somewhere. I'd worked so hard for years building my career at Purdue. I was exactly where I wanted to be, and I loved the work I was doing. I wasn't about to give that up without a real fight. Here's what I said to myself: "OK, Virginia, you're losing your sight, so what do you need to be doing to get the job done, regardless?" "Whether?" wasn't a question I ever asked, not once. "How?" was what concerned me.

I'm not sure where my faith—and my religion—fit into the equation, but I'm sure that it helped me rise to the challenge and not just collapse and give up when I knew I was going blind. I'm a practicing Roman Catholic, almost never miss Mass, but I don't wear it on my sleeve, and I certainly don't preach about it. It's just there, always, and I know it makes a difference, probably in two really important ways. For one thing, I sincerely believe that God has given me certain gifts that I'm obligated to put to good use in my life, no matter what barriers I have to get over. And I also really do believe that events happen for a reason—in some way they're God-given—and the challenges that come my way aren't just accidental, they're part of some kind of cosmic plan. I know that might sound a little like I'm heading across the border into la-la land, but it worked—and still works—for me to think of my blindness as having purpose, more than just a horrible blow, and it's my job to figure out the purpose. That's the way it's worked out, anyway, so why not believe that? By the way, I probably say little prayers ten times a day or more. Maybe it's a kind of crutch, I don't know, but it's helped me get through some rough times, that's all I know, so it's a good crutch.

I hope that doesn't sound arrogant, and I don't want to give the impression that it was easy to keep going as my sight steadily got worse, but I didn't see any choice; I just had to do whatever it took. I did, by the way, begin to educate myself on blindness and the resources available to the blind, including new technologies, of course, but also education and training. I made a real effort to get to know blind students at Purdue, attended several of their functions, and I got myself appointed to a couple of boards: the Indiana Public Television Reading Information Service and a social services agency that had technology for the visually impaired. I also learned about the Miami Lighthouse for the Blind through my daughter Julie, who was teaching at Florida International University, specializing in human/computer interaction, designing interfaces, things like that.

Julie and I were talking one day, and I came up with the idea that she should write a proposal to the National Science Foundation to develop ways of adapting computers to particular kinds of vision impairment. Like, I've got retinitis pigmentosa, so the computer monitor shouldn't have stuff on the periphery, but if I've got macular degeneration, the monitor shouldn't have stuff in the middle. And there's the question of coming up with the right color contrast. Julie followed through, got a really prestigious NSF Presidential Career Award, amounting to a half-million dollars. She linked up with the Miami Lighthouse because she needed low-vision subjects to study. So I knew quite a bit about the Lighthouse before I ever imagined enrolling there.

A real step forward, where my blindness IQ was concerned, was when the governor of Indiana called Purdue's president or provost, I can't recall exactly who, and said something like, "You guys always say that you don't have any money for state mandates, and yet there's Perkins [Carl D. Perkins Vocational and Technical Education Act] money for people with special needs and you guys haven't submitted anything." Well, I was talking with the president and provost about this after the call, and they said if we wanted any Perkins money we had to get the proposal in the next day. I said, "Let me write something." It really wasn't my job to write proposals, but I knew this was a great opportunity to take my knowledge to the next level. There was a blind woman in the dean of student's office. So I went over there to see her, and I said, "Nancy, I want to write a proposal, and if you're a blind student what do you need in order to be able to succeed at Purdue, and what don't we have?" She was generous enough to take the trouble to educate me. And so I went back to my office. I typed up something. I went back to see her, and I said, "Take a look at this and tell me what you think. Do I have this right? Did I miss anything here?" So I came up with this idea that Purdue would have an ALPS lab. That means "Adaptive Learning Programs," which, by the way, is often called "assistive technology." This would be the location where students with disabilities, primarily visual impairment because that was what I was interested in, could go for special education. There'd be tutors, and the right equipment and software. Writing the proposal is how I first learned about technologies like JAWS, ZoomText, and Dragon Dictate that we'll talk about later.

So I wrote the proposal, and that morning I called the governor's office and explained my idea for an ALPS lab at Purdue. But the person I was talking with said, "Remember: the Perkins money is reserved for two-year students." And I said, "What if we say that it's for students in our two-year programs who are working on associate degrees—that they'd have first priority, but in the event that the equipment isn't being used, rather than have it sitting idle, anyone could use it?" Being told that would be fine, I talked with the deans who headed Purdue's two two-year programs about their needs. For example one of our two programs was in veterinary medicine, so I called the dean over there, and I said, "Do you have any visually impaired students?" He said, "Yes, we have one." And I said, "What's the biggest problem?" And he said, "Using the microscope." And I said, "Well, is there any kind of a microscope that magnifies enough for this student?" He said, "Yes, but we can't afford it." I said, "Get me the specs. I'm going to put it in a proposal." So I stuck that in there. Anyway, the proposal got funded, and that was the beginning of the ALPS Lab at Purdue. I subsequently made a point of getting acquainted with the lab's director, who was a blind mechanical engineer. He was one of a small number of people at Purdue I told about my retinitis pigmentosa, and on my visits to the lab I'd ask him how this or that piece of equipment was used, so it was a great learning opportunity.

I also wanted to know more about education and training opportunities for blind adults, which, by the way, falls in the area of vocational rehabilitation. So I called the state office handling vocational rehabilitation, saying "I'm losing my vision (I didn't tell them who I was, of course) and I'd like to know how this vocational rehabilitation thing works." And they said, "First you've got to get a hearing test, then you've got to have a physical, then you need to take a psychological test," and I'm thinking, "All I really want to know is, when you lose your eyesight, what's there for you? What do you use?" So I discounted that, I wasn't going there. You know, when I looked into vocational rehabilitation programs for the blind in Indiana as part of what you might call my intelligence gathering, it was pretty depressing. Things might have changed since then, but when I was looking, my only option was what's called a "sheltered workshop," where I'd be learning such practical skills as basket weaving, caning, things like that. I thought about myself going through something like that, and I just couldn't imagine it. Now, don't get me wrong, I'm not saying that sheltered workshops aren't a wonderful resource for many people with disabilities; they certainly are. But my needs were obviously very different.

There's another thing that comes to me that's really amazing. Not one of the doctors I talked with about my condition during my Purdue years said anything about the resources that I might take advantage of as my sight slowly but surely disappeared. No medical person ever said, "Virginia, you're such a successful professional, you need to think about this program, or that new technology so you can continue to contribute." Nothing like that, absolutely nothing. What I heard was, "There's nothing more we can do for you." I don't want to get ahead of our story, but I just want to say that we're fighting that kind of thing at the Miami Lighthouse, mainly by getting the word out as widely as we can to medical professionals. It's really sad, when you think of all the creative people who've given up hope over the years, gotten deeply depressed, because of that sort of negative, hopeless diagnosis!

## DOUG:

Tell me more about how you dealt with your advancing blindness beyond educating yourself, Virginia. How were you able to keep up with a tremendously demanding job?

## VIRGINIA:

I had two very clear goals, Doug. First, I intended be as effective at doing my job as I always had, no matter what extra time and effort it would take. I had no intention of asking for any special favors because I was going blind. And second, I wanted to keep my condition under wraps for as long as I feasibly could. I'm not a paranoid person, never have been, never will be, but I've always thought of myself as a realist, and you'd have to be incredibly naïve to believe that there wouldn't be someone in a bureaucracy as large as Purdue's who would be tempted to take advantage of a person in a key, very visible position who was losing her eyesight. Keeping the secret added a whole additional layer of complexity to my coping strategies.

Before giving you some examples, I've got to acknowledge the role that Bob and my kids played in keeping me in the game at Purdue as my eyesight gradually got worse. I couldn't possibly have succeeded as well as I did without their constant encouragement and very practical support. For example, you'll recall that I never drove again after that incident on the way to the beauty salon when I hit and dragged those wooden horses through the intersection. So Bob and I would drive to work together, and whenever possible, he'd drive me home. And if he couldn't, I'd catch a cab. But I never caught the cab outside Hovde Hall, I'd walk to Stewart Center instead, where there was a cab stand. And whenever I had to take a cab to work, I'd have the driver drop me off a block away from Hovde so I wouldn't have to answer any questions about why I wasn't driving.

My three kids were always ready to jump in when I needed them, in little and big ways. The other day I was talking with my son, Robert, who was in college when things were going downhill on the vision front, and he reminded me about taking over his own laundry when he'd come home for visits. "I started doing my own laundry and not leaving it for you, partly because I didn't want you worrying about it, you had enough on your mind. But, to be completely honest, I also didn't want my shirts in the hamper with yours for fear you'd throw them in with the wrong colors, or not pre-spot a stain." And, just like Bob, the kids were also ready to serve as chauffeurs when needs be. I remember one day I was walking back to Hovde Hall from the beauty salon, when I got caught in a tremendous downpour, and I was drenched. A friend of my kids saw me, and shouted from his apartment door, "Mrs. Jacko, are you trying to win the wet tee shirt contest?" When I got back to the office, I called the kids, and one of them ran home to get me another outfit to wear. These kinds of things happened every now and then. Thank heaven, we lived only a mile or so from the campus.

Getting around a campus as large as Purdue was a big challenge, of course. I did walk to meetings, but in some neighborhoods I went through there were intersections I had to cross without stoplights, and I couldn't see ongoing cars until they were pretty close, so I suppose I now and then took my life in my hands. Thank heaven, Purdue's in a pretty slow-moving college town, not at all like Miami with its nonstop, frenetic traffic. I would wear a hat with a visor so I would have more contrast on my walks, but then I'd stick the visor in my briefcase when I got close to Hovde Hall. And since I made a lot of presentations in different locations all over the campus, I had to worry about the rooms themselves, not just how to get to them. If I hadn't been in a room before, I'd have Bob walk me over an hour or so before my meeting so I could get a feel for the room and not "look blind." I'd want to walk in the room appearing as confident as possible, but when you're slowly losing your eyesight, even though you might see things in the room, there's kind of a delayed reaction. You look around until your brain picks things up, so you can avoid that delayed reaction—that blind look—by spending some time in the room beforehand.

Naturally, there were things I just couldn't prepare for, like walking by someone without saying anything because I didn't see them. This is what happened with a person I'd recently hired. We both attended a workshop at Stewart Center, and in our next one-on-one meeting, she said, "Virginia, did I do something wrong?" I said, "What do you mean?" And she said, "Well, when we were standing in the hall at the break, you never came over to say 'hi' to me." And now and then people would notice little accidents, like my bumping against the edge of a table on the way back to my seat after a presentation. I later learned that someone who'd seen that happen to me wondered if I was having eye trouble of some kind. So it was a constant battle to keep people from knowing, or even suspecting, that I was losing my sight.

To take another, funnier example, since my staff was spread all around the campus, we had weekly brown bag lunch meetings in Hovde Hall. On one Monday morning, I started my day by—proudly—making my own ham sandwich, and I reached into the refrigerator for a can of diet Coke and put them in a brown bag for that day's lunch meeting. But I'd forgotten that my brother, who'd visited us that weekend, had brought his own cans of Budweiser because he knew we were not beer drinkers, and he'd left a few cans of beer next to the diet Coke. So at 11:45, I went into the conference room and put my lunch bag and supposed can of Coke on the table. I then left the conference room and, having a few minutes to spare, went down the hall to talk with the provost. When I returned to the conference room all of my staff were seated waiting, looking at the can of beer by my brown bag. Purdue was one of those universities that banned alcohol on campus, by the way. After greeting everyone, I began to pop the tab on my can when the business manager for libraries, sitting next to me, said, "Virginia, are we allowed to have beer at our brown bag lunches?" In a flash, I recalled, oh, my, Bill left some beer in our refrigerator and I couldn't tell the difference. I immediately chuckled and said, "Oh, it was dark this morning when I made my lunch and I didn't want to wake anyone up so I didn't turn on the kitchen light and must have grabbed the wrong can." The best laid plans . . . !

But as time passed, I did confide in a few people who were really helpful. For example, we'd have a council of academic officers' luncheon once a month. It included the provost, sometimes the president, and all the vice presidents and deans. I was the only non-dean who went to those luncheons, and they were always a buffet. I hated buffets because, you know, the corn kind of looked like the mashed potatoes—stuff like that—and you could easily make a dumb-looking mistake. So I made a point of getting to know one of the vice presidents, a biologist doing retina research, and I eventually confided in him: "Luis, I'm starting to lose my eyesight. I've got retinitis pigmentosa, and I just don't want people to know about it yet." So when I would go to the council of academic officers' luncheon every month I'd always get in line with him, and then he's say, "Oh, Virginia, let me take your plate and help you." Things like that. And so you had a few people that you really trusted.

In light of the pretty wide range of responsibilities I had at Hovde Hall, preparing for meetings was in a league by itself—easily my toughest challenge. I spent hours and hours at night and on weekends making sure I was so prepared that no one who wasn't already in the know would suspect that I couldn't see normally. I'd go over spreadsheets at home with a fine-tooth comb, with my head close to the page, before meetings, getting a mental picture in my mind and memorizing the key numbers, so in the meeting I could sit and talk with you about everything and you wouldn't have a clue that I couldn't clearly see all the numbers on the page. And, believe me, you never saw me my head bent over the page "looking blind."

One of the most demanding meetings was the president's mid-year management reviews with all of the academic schools. I'd have to meet with the people on the business side of those ten schools and tell them that the president and provost were especially interested in looking at things like enrollment, the number of presidential scholars and NSF scholarships, grant dollars per full-time-equivalent faculty—parameters like that. Then I'd instruct them to get me the information a week in advance so I'd have time to prepare myself for the meetings and summarize the key facts for the president and provost. Being in control of the schedule really helped since I could space out the preparation. So I would say to myself, "Okay, I'm going to be certain that a small school, Pharmacy for example, goes before Liberal Arts, which was huge. And then we'll have another small school like Nursing, and then we'll have Engineering which is big," so that I would have the time to prepare. If all the big ones had been bunched together, my job would have been much, much harder, if not impossible.

I got to the point that I couldn't use the computer at Purdue, so I hired a techie, who sat in the office right next to mine, to do all of my computer work. And toward the very end at Purdue, I got a CCTV, which enabled me to read documents on a monitor and adjust the contrast for easier reading. That would have been my last six months since it would have sent a signal to people, "Oh, Virginia needs accessible stuff," you know. By then, I didn't really have a choice since it gave me the visual field I needed to read. Bob, always my guardian angel, came by my office one day when I was using the CCTV, and he said "Don't look like that" when he saw me sitting pigeon-toed with my bent head close to the monitor. He also had me move my desk, which had been facing the door, so that people coming into my office would see my side profile and not notice me straining to read the monitor.

I began to see the handwriting on the wall when Purdue got a new purchasing system that involved us doing all of the approvals on the computer. The trouble was, when you brought the program up on the monitor, it was all graphical, and not accessible for a visually impaired person. You didn't like just bring up a window and go to approvals, which is something that would be more text based. It was highly graphical, and I realized there wasn't any way that I could approve anything on the system. This really did feel like some kind of tipping point, but I didn't know where it was tipping to. I knew that I'd have to ask my secretary to handle the approvals, and that definitely wasn't the way it was supposed to work.

Talking about the lighter side of keeping up appearances, Doug, I went to every Purdue football game even though I couldn't see what was happening on the field; I loved college football, and I wanted to be there, with the crowd and the excitement, so I carried a radio with me to the games. Bob and I even went to a game at Ohio State, and since they didn't allow radios in the stadium, Bob smuggled mine in under his jacket; now there's a saint for you!

**DOUG:**

You tried to keep your condition under wraps as long as possible. When did you tell the powers that be in Hovde Hall that you were losing your sight?

**VIRGINIA:**

If I recall correctly, I told the treasurer I had retinitis pigmentosa in 1999, and he told the other officers at Hovde Hall, so it was around a year before I took medical leave to enroll at the Miami Lighthouse. Here's how it happened. You remember I told you about attending a workshop with a woman I'd just hired and not seeing her in the hallway during a break? Well, that was a wakeup call. That night I said to Bob, "I think I've got to go see a lawyer because I don't have a clue what will happen if the big boys get wind of my problem. We can't afford not to know where I'll be standing legally once they learn about what's going on." So I went to see a social security lawyer. It was a real milestone in my life because he said to me, "Look, have you told your boss that you've got this prognosis that you're going to lose your eyesight leading to total blindness?" I said, "No, because I'm not sure how they'd handle hearing that." He said, "Well, before they make you business manager of the janitors you have to sit down with your boss and say, 'I've got this problem,' because then you're protected under the ADA [the federal Americans with Disabilities Act]. But if you don't inform them, tomorrow they could say, 'What's wrong with Virginia? Is she drinking or something?' " So, I set up a meeting with the treasurer. That's when I guess you could say it was official. By the way, he responded really positively: "Oh, Virginia, we hired you for your brains, not your eyes. There's nothing to worry about."

To tell the truth, Doug, I didn't take this at face value, since I've always lived in the real world. So when people occasionally ask me, "Don't you wish you'd have told him sooner?" my response is always "Never!" I knew that if the word that I was going blind got around widely, I would've had a much, much more difficult time doing my job, and I probably couldn't have lasted nearly as long as I did. I don't think it was far-fetched to worry that people would think differently about me, which I truly to this day believe does happen to people. That's why I pushed myself so far, worked so hard—so people wouldn't think I was losing my sight. By the time I took medical leave the people who worked closest with me in Hovde Hall knew, and there were a few others, like the vice president who'd helped me at the buffet and the blind engineer at the ALPS lab, but only a handful. There were times I just needed to share what was going on, of course. I had a good friend, the business manager for the business school, who was my closest business colleague. She was slowly dying of cancer. One day, she picked me up to drive to a meeting together, and she was telling me about her diagnosis, when I on the spur of the moment told her what was going on with me. But that was the real exception to the rule.

Keeping my condition secret really kept me on my toes, as you'd imagine; I had to watch myself constantly. To take an example, I couldn't afford to use a calculator in meetings, for two reasons: I'd have to get real close to the screen, and any glare would making seeing numbers impossible, no matter how close I got. So I became extremely good at mental math. The provost and I would be talking, and he would say, "Okay, now if we do salary raises, and if we increase salaries by 3%, but we have an additional 1% market increase, but we only increase student fees by 2%, how much more additional revenue are we going to have to raise?" And I knew what my base was, because when I would look at a number I would never say "one hundred eighty-nine million six hundred and thirty-six thousand five hundred." I would say to myself "189.6 million = 190 million." And so when I would go into a meeting I would always have that round number in my mind, so that if we would say, "Well, if we do 2% on this, 1% on that," very quickly I could say, "Oh, well that's going to cost you another twenty million dollars." And he would look at me, and he'd say, "Now wait a minute." He'd get his calculator out, and he would do it. He'd punch all the numbers through, and then he'd say, "How in heaven's name did you do that?"

I also learned to pay close attention to my facial expressions and body language so that I didn't inadvertently communicate my vision problem. I really do think that as my sight got increasingly worse, I would occasionally sort of retreat into myself, kind of disengage, and I'd now and then let myself lose eye contact with people in meetings. I don't do that now, as CEO of the Lighthouse, as you've observed. I'm always looking directly at you and other people I'm talking with in meetings. But back then I wasn't as aware of the danger of disengaging, so I'd sometimes get caught off guard. I remember being in a meeting with the provost one day, when he said, "You disagree with me, don't you?" I said, "No, I don't." He said, "I know you do. I can tell by your face." And I thought to myself, "What am I doing, because I really don't disagree with him." Thinking about it later, I realized that I had probably let myself retreat into my own inner world for a moment, and he interpreted it as disagreement. My husband, Bob, has always been a great help by pointing such moments out to me.

**DOUG:**

Tell me about making the decision to go on medical leave and enroll yourself at the Miami Lighthouse in January 2001.

## VIRGINIA:

Well in August of 2000 Purdue appointed a new president from Iowa State, so I was a total stranger to him. I'm thinking, "Gosh, I ought to mention my condition." So I asked the provost what the president knew about my eye problem, and he said, "I told him that you had retinitis pigmentosa, but that you're doing a great job for us." But I could sense that a new era was beginning; the players were starting to change, and I was faced with having to build new relationships, starting with the president. Anyway, I was scheduled to meet with the new president in November to go over material for the mid-December management review meeting. As always, I'd spent the evening before making sure I was in command of the facts and would appear on top of my game, no fumbling around. Outside the president's office, at the opposite end from my office were big glass doors, and the secretary, Nancy, was in the back, and there was a conference room on the side.

So I'm standing at Nancy's desk, when she takes me aside and says, "Virginia, he got all new furniture this weekend." I said, "Oh, well, what's it like?" And she said, "Oh, it's really beautiful. All glass, very nice." And I'm thinking, "Glass?" I said, "Well, has it got framework around it?" She said, "Oh, no. Real modern." I said, "Is anything in the same place." She said, "No, it's totally rearranged." And I said, "I think I'm going to have trouble." She said, "I'll tell you what, if I tell the president you're not ready and offer him a coke, he'll have to go to the bathroom after he has the coke. I'm going to tell him you're not ready to meet with him, and when he goes to the bathroom I'll show you around the room." So I said, "Okay, tell him I'm not ready," even though that really grated on my nerves since I always prided myself on being prepared to the hilt and on time. Anyway, it goes according to plan, and Nancy pops out to tell me he's in his private bathroom and she'll show me around the rearranged office.

So I go in there, and I realize I don't see the edges of the coffee table. I don't see this modern desk. I don't see the conference table that used to be there. And I can see there's a big L-shaped sofa. And I say, "Nancy, do you mind telling the president that you've seated me." She said, "We normally don't do that." "That's okay, Nancy," I said. "Just tell him that you've seated me on his sofa." So he walks back in from the bathroom, and I'm sitting there. I say "hi," stand up, shake his hand, and say "I've got some items to go over for the management review meeting that's coming up." He and I are sitting there on his L-shaped sofa talking, and I'm thinking, "When I get up to walk out of here I have to walk really wide because I don't have a clue where the glass coffee table is." And as I'm leaving his office I say to myself, "This can't go on. You've got to do things differently."

So, getting back to my office, I shut the door and called my husband, Bob, and I said, "Bob, you know that sabbatical at the University of Miami? How difficult would it be for you to get it in time for us to be in Miami by January 5?" He said, "I'll call right away and give you a call back." He called back a few minutes later to say, "Yeah, I can start in January." I said, "Okay, I'm going to call the Miami Lighthouse for the Blind and see if I can start their program in January." After hearing back from the Lighthouse that, yes, they could enroll me in their vocational rehabilitation program that coming January, I went across the hall to talk with the treasurer. "You know I'm losing my eyesight," I said. "Well, I need to get some new skills so I can keep up with my job, so I'm applying for a three-month medical leave and enrolling at the Miami Lighthouse for the Blind." He was supportive. Indeed, when I'd first told him about the retinitis pigmentosa, he'd said, "I hope you're doing something for yourself."

By the time of the mid-December management review meeting, which is the last meeting I attended at Purdue, I'd been accepted as a student at the Miami Lighthouse, beginning on January 5. Purdue had granted me a three-month medical leave, and I had a person appointed to fill my position on an interim basis until I returned from Miami. Bob and I spent Christmas in Miami, at the condo we'd bought years earlier for our kids to use while they were living there.

I mentioned earlier that I never for a minute considered submitting my resignation at Purdue since, as far as I was concerned, I'd be returning to my old job. After all, there was ADA [the Americans with Disabilities Act] to protect me, so why wouldn't I return to take up where I'd left off, only with some new skills to help me perform even better? That's not the way it worked out, of course, and in retrospect, what ended up happening was a true blessing, for which I'll always be grateful. Now, looking back nine years later, I realize that I almost certainly couldn't have returned and just picked up where I'd left off at Purdue. I couldn't have been as influential as before—not even close. That chapter in my life was over, though I didn't know it then. I was headed in a dramatic new direction on my professional and personal journey, and I'd pretty soon find a new mission I felt much more passionate about—to guide me and make my life even more rewarding, despite the fact that I was going blind. We've talked about Viktor Frankl's concept of meaning and Joseph Campbell's "bliss" [Reader:

See Postscript 2]. Well, my life in less than a year would become much more meaningful than it'd ever been, and I'd discover bliss that I'd never imagined.

# PART TWO

## THE MIAMI LIGHTHOUSE: PERSONAL AND PROFESSIONAL REBIRTH

### DOUG'S OVERVIEW

Accompanied by her husband, Bob, daughter Julie, and son-in-law, Francois, in early January 2001, Virginia Jacko arrived at the Miami Lighthouse for the Blind and Visually Impaired to begin her vocational rehabilitation program. Having been granted a medical leave from Purdue University, she intended to return to her senior financial position at Hovde Hall after completing her training at the Lighthouse. Better armed to function as a blind executive, Virginia would, she thought, pick up where she had left off, once again working directly with Purdue's president, provost, treasurer and other senior executives. Virginia was committed to making the most of her vocational rehabilitation program at the Lighthouse, so she approached this new challenge with her customary drive and tenacity. Over the course of her three-month Lighthouse program, in addition to learning Braille and acquiring essential personal living skills, Virginia received mobility training and became familiar with the latest computer applications for the blind.

During one of Virginia's mobility lessons at the Lighthouse, her instructor recommended that she get a guide dog, which would require her to spend a fourth month away from Purdue at guide dog school in New York. It made the best of sense. Not only was Virginia physically fit enough to exercise a dog, she would have more security and mobility than a white cane could offer. However, this was anything but simple decision to make since Virginia knew that she could not extend her medical leave from Purdue for another month. She had no doubt that guide dog training would make her a higher functioning blind person, ultimately expanding her personal and professional horizons, but the short-term price would be extraordinary. Not only would Virginia be giving up an influential position and the concomitant professional status that she had worked tremendously hard to build over her twenty-plus years at Purdue, she would also be losing a source of immense satisfaction and pride; indeed she would be stripping away a large piece of the self-image that she had created over the years. And this very substantial bird-in-hand would be exchanged for a future seen only through a glass darkly. If Virginia decided to leave Purdue, she would begin the next phase of her journey without a clear professional vision to guide her or detailed professional goals to shoot for. Not one to agonize over complex decisions, Virginia once again acted decisively, resigning from Purdue and setting out on a new journey headed she knew not where.

At the end of June 2001, when Virginia completed guide dog training in New York, she faced another important decision. She was told she needed to spend two months in one place with her new dog, Tracker, so where would she be: back home in Indiana with Bob, who had to return to his teaching duties at Purdue on August 1, or at their condo in Miami? With Bob's strong encouragement, Virginia decided to remain in Miami for the next two months. Of course, you would not have seen Virginia lounging by the condo pool during the two months she spent in Miami with Tracker. Being Virginia, she was a perpetual motion machine, devoting the bulk of her time to volunteering at the Lighthouse, starting a guide dog group and speaking about the Lighthouse at schools and service organizations around Miami.

Then it was back to Indiana and her home with Bob in the early fall. They lived way out in the country far from everything and everyone, and for the first time in years, Virginia had neither a job nor a mission to challenge her mentally and consume her tremendous energy. This uncustomary new life quickly proved unsatisfying, and Virginia, with Bob's strong backing, began to alternate between West Lafayette and Miami, eventually spending the bulk of her time in Miami, becoming an even more active and visible Lighthouse volunteer. So Virginia was a near-permanent Miami resident by 2004, when she was appointed to the Lighthouse Board of Directors and not long after was elected treasurer of the Board.

Virginia's successful stint as treasurer of a major nonprofit institution, with at that time thirty-five employees and a budget of about $3 million, was undoubtedly why the Lighthouse Board unanimously accepted her offer to serve as interim president and CEO, on a pro bono basis, in February 2005, when the president who had originally approached her about serving on the Board resigned. Interestingly, back in 2001, while still a vocational rehabilitation student, Virginia had briefly considered throwing her hat in the ring when the Lighthouse president and CEO position had come open, but had been strongly discouraged. However, in 2005, both Virginia and the Lighthouse were in a very different place. She had thoroughly mastered the software to read Excel spreadsheets, using assistive software she had learned as a Lighthouse student, clearly demonstrating to her Board colleagues during her term as treasurer that she was in command of intricate financial details, and her self-confidence as a blind executive had grown by the day.

Having conducted a thorough national CEO search, the Lighthouse Board named Virginia permanent president and CEO in June 2005, on the basis of her impressive stint as interim CEO, and since becoming CEO Virginia has built an outstanding track record. One of the most notable accomplishments on her watch has been the Lighthouse's acquisition of the Heiken Children's Vision Program, including its mobile vision care vans, which are fully equipped optometric offices on wheels that travel to schools in low-income areas. The transformation of the Lighthouse Board into a much more effective governing body under her leadership is discussed in Postscript 1. Virginia has also overseen the launching of a number of new Lighthouse programs since taking the helm, including music production, ceramics, hot lunches for clients, fitness, and a low-vision center. One important sign of the Lighthouse's success under Virginia's leadership is its receiving Charity Navigator's highest four-star designation two years in a row, signaling that the Lighthouse is among the nation's most effective nonprofits.

Virginia has also been a consummate fund-raiser, nurturing the largest single-donor gifts in the Lighthouse's history: two incentive matching gifts of over $1 million each from prominent Miami businesswomen and philanthropists, which have funded the new third floor children's wing, the state-of-the-art sound studio, and a music inclusion program for talented blind and sighted young adults, and have supplemented general operating funds. She has become a prominent member of the Greater Miami community, being chosen as the South Florida Business Journal's 2007 Business Woman of the Year in the Nonprofit Leader category and receiving the 2008 Quiet Storm Achiever Award in the nonprofit category from the South Florida Women's Power Caucus, among many other honors.

Now Virginia can flesh out this account of her Lighthouse years in her own words.

## DOUG AND VIRGINIA IN CONVERSATION

### DOUG:

Tell me about your feelings as you arrived at the Lighthouse in January 2001. You must have had some misgivings as you jumped into a totally strange milieu.

### VIRGINIA:

Well, there was a lot going on inside me then, as you might imagine. One side of me was determined to charge ahead, no matter what, without looking back. You might think this sounds weird, but I really did believe I was on a journey, and I said to myself, "I don't know where this journey's going to take me. I don't know for sure where I'm going, where this road's going, but I embrace it." And I really did want to embrace it. When I went to Hovde Hall I always wore a St.

John knit and a pair of real high heels, and now I'm coming to the Lighthouse, and I'm like, "But you're going to be walking down the street with a cane." So I said to myself, "Okay, well I guess I've got to buy some nice tennis shoes and a nice pair of slacks." One of my staff reminded me the other day that I arrived every day during training looking very nice, very sporty, although that wasn't how I'd liked to dress at Purdue—I'd always had a business-formal look. But I said, "You know what? You're just going to have to do that. You can't afford to fail." So, you charge ahead, you don't have any choice. I mean, if you've got a lot of choices, then you can be picky. But what was I going to do? I didn't see any alternative to the Lighthouse. Believe me, I looked in Indiana, as I've said before. For many people with disabilities, a sheltered workshop is a wonderful resource, does a world of good, but it wasn't a real choice for me.

But being determined doesn't mean I wasn't scared that first day when I arrived at the Lighthouse. My husband, Bob, is driving me, and my son-in-law Francois's sitting in the back seat with me, and my daughter Julie's in the front seat with Bob. And I'm not a touchy-feely person. I mean, you know that down here everyone's hugging everybody else and all that. That doesn't mean I love people less, it's just not my style. So anyway, I'm sitting there in the back seat, and I'm suddenly thinking to myself, "What the heck am I doing here? What am I getting into?" And I reached over, and I grabbed Francois' thigh, and I just squeezed it so hard all the way to the Lighthouse. I'm sure he was wondering what was going on. When we got to the Lighthouse, Bob turned around and said to Francois, "Gee, it didn't seem to bother her at all." And Francois said, "Oh, yeah it did. I could tell.

She was hanging on for dear life." So anyway, when I walked through those doors I was saying to myself, "God, I hope they can help me," but I didn't really have a clue. I just couldn't see an alternative, and so that was that.

**DOUG:**

So you've walked through the Lighthouse doors, and you've begun a new journey. Talk about your vocational rehabilitation experience.

**VIRGINIA:**

First thing, I was told I needed to meet with the social worker, and I'm thinking, "Social worker? I don't need a social worker. Just tell me what class I'm supposed to go to." And so I sat down with the social worker, who was doing an assessment, and she asked me what my goals were. And so I thought to myself, "What do I really want to do?" You're going to laugh at the first thing that came to my mind. "You know," I told her, "I don't cook as much for my husband. I'd like to know how to make cookies and not burn them. How do you know when your cookies are done if you can't see them?" So she checked off what they call "Personal Management." By the way, this turned out to be tremendously important because you feel like you're losing control if you're not able to do little personal things at home that you used to take for granted. You don't want to be dependent on other people for simple things like baking cookies. Really early in my training I said to one of my instructors, "It's so frustrating. I lose a button, and I can't even sew it back on." She said, "You can sew a button on." I said, "But how?" So she showed me how to use a special needle that the Lighthouse sells in its store, and I thought, "Oh my God, I can even sew a button on again." It was really liberating—learning how to do such a small, everyday thing—and I can't tell you how much I appreciate all of the practical personal living skills I picked up in my Lighthouse training.

When the social worker asked about Braille, it sounded like something that only blind people would do, and I guess I couldn't yet see myself becoming a completely blind person. So I said, "No, no, I don't need Braille." After I was here just a couple of days I had second thoughts about that. "Why aren't you going to learn Braille?" I said to myself. "It's just like a foreign language you'll be needing someday." So then I came back down to the social worker's office, and told her I wanted to learn Braille, too. She said, "Well, it takes a long time." I said, "That's okay. I have three months. I'm on a three-month medical leave, and I've got to learn all of this stuff in three months, so now I want Braille, too." You know, I never did become really fluent in Braille, I've stayed at a beginner level, but even my elementary knowledge has turned out to be quite valuable. Just to take a small example before we go on, I use Braille labels on my folders, so in meetings I can easily come up with the papers I need without fumbling around, that kind of thing.

What I was most concerned about was learning to use the computer as a blind person, since at this point I couldn't even do a spreadsheet any longer. I'll say more about that later, but I want to tell you about my amusing confrontation with the powers-that-be early in my student days. I was on a mission and wasn't about to waste any precious time, so when I was told that I needed to take typing before I could study computing, I raised a real ruckus. "Oh, no." I said, "I'm already a top-notch typist." My social worker said, "No, you have to be in typing," and she told me I'd be scheduled for two typing slots, one in the morning and one in the afternoon. I objected, "I don't need that. I want computing right away." And she said, "No, it doesn't work that way." I said, "Okay." So I go to my typing class, and I'm like, "Okay, this is ridiculous. I know how to type. Why am I doing this?" So I go back, and I see my social worker, and I say, "You know, I really don't want typing."

And I was told, "Well, we're sorry, but that's the way it's done." So I'm in typing for a week, and I say to the instructor, "How can I arrange to take an exam so that I can be finished with my typing?" And he said, "Well, we really don't do that." And I said, "Well, there must be an exam." He said, "Well, there really isn't." My response: "This is a problem. I've only got three months, and I'm wasting two hours a day, and I just can't waste two hours a day, so if you can't get me out of typing I'm going to have to call the Division of Blind Services and ask them to change the schedule." I didn't know it at the time, but this was a real hot button; they didn't want me calling the state funding agency because it was footing a lot of the training bill. So the next day I had a new schedule with computing twice a day. Thank heaven I didn't make myself persona non grata! But, you know, I didn't think I had a choice; my time was precious and all-too-limited, and I just couldn't afford to sit through useless classes. Of course, this kind of experience has proved to be very valuable to me as the Lighthouse CEO, but that hadn't entered my mind then.

Two technological advances that I took advantage of in my Lighthouse training have made a huge difference to me professionally: the note taker and JAWS. I'm a bit ashamed to say that I resisted learning both of them at first. I was taking a felt-tip marker and notebook to my Braille class, and I'd write down "cell one equals a, cell one and two equal b," etc., and one day the instructor came over and asked what I was doing. When I said, "Well I'm writing this stuff down so I can go home and memorize it," she said, "But you've got retinitis pigmentosa, and you're not going to be able to read that eventually, so you really need to get a note taker." I didn't know what she was referring to, but she was one of those angels who've passed through my life, and the note taker has made a huge difference. A note taker is basically a keyboard with a computer chip in it, and since you don't need a monitor, it's really small. I've got one right on my desk, and that's how I take notes in meetings. The way it works, you type what's being said in a meeting, using the keyboard, and you're able to listen to auditory feedback, which is what I do, or read a Braille display. I don't know what I'd do without it.

Because I still had vision, impaired as it was, when I was going through my vocational rehabilitation program at the Lighthouse, I wanted to learn how to use the screen enhancement software called ZoomText, rather than JAWS, which is designed for people who are totally blind. Fortunately for me, the Lighthouse didn't have any ZoomText instructors, but had a slot available in a JAWS class. JAWS, which stands for "job application with speech," is a screen reading software that tells the blind person what's on the screen based upon the key stroke commands that you use. So, for example, on a full keyboard there's the number pad over here, and you can do "numlock on" or "numlock off," depending on whether or not you want to use it as a number keypad. You control JAWS a lot through that keypad by memorizing a bunch of key strokes. For example, if you want to know what letter the cursor's on in a document you're reading, you hit the number 5 key, and the computer tells you. If you want to know the next word, you hit the insert key and the number 6. If you want to know what the word is before the number 5 where the cursor is, then you hit insert and number 4. If you want to go to the top of a document, you hit the insert key with the home key. If you want to go to the bottom of the document, you hit the insert key with the end key. Or, you can command the computer to read the whole document to you.

It's an amazing advance for blind people who are able to learn all of the keystrokes you need for the different operations, in programs like Word, Excel, and Outlook. For example, I can listen to email messages, open and listen to attachments, edit attachments, reply to emails—anything a sighted person can do. So the playing field is really leveled using JAWS, and it's a real blessing that I didn't end up wasting time learning ZoomText, since I certainly wouldn't be using it now that I'm totally blind. I've asked myself if maybe this is another example of fate at work in my life: the wrong thing I wanted to study wasn't available, but the right thing I didn't want to study was. I definitely lucked out.

I can't tell you how much urgency I was feeling during my training program. The way I saw it then, I'd be headed back to Purdue in only three months, and that was my window for mastering Braille and all the other stuff I needed, like JAWS. I didn't know how things would be when I got back to Purdue, whether there'd be a big ADA issue of some kind, but I was sure that, if I nailed the content in my classes, I'd be better at my job than when I left on medical leave, so the stakes were sky-high. This meant that I was kind of like the class nerd. I'm a real people person, and I truly enjoyed being with my classmates, but I always felt like there was just barely enough time to learn what I needed to learn, so while the other students were having lunch or walking in the park together, I'd be sitting in the courtyard going over my lessons. It was worth the effort, though the payoff certainly wasn't what I expected it would be at the time.

I'll never forget one of the most important events—a real turning point—in my Lighthouse student days. I wanted to be able to walk from my condo to a park around three blocks away, along a very busy street, Bayshore Drive, so my mobility instructor had been working with me on this. One day he said, "You're ready, Virginia. Today, I'm going to go ahead to the park and wait for you, and you're going to make the trip on your own." You can't believe how exhilarating it was, doing it on my own, tapping with my cane, feeling a rock here, knowing it's going to change to grass, and then it's going to change to pebbles, and then there's going to be an intersection, and then you're going through the intersection. You've practiced and practiced, you've got the route mapped out in your mind, and then you're actually doing it on your own. When I made it to the park, I started to cry, I was so happy. I'd made it to the park by myself! It really worked with the cane! I heard my instructor get out of his car, and I thought, "God, I can't let him know I'm crying. Get yourself together pronto, Virginia, or he'll think you're losing it." When he came up to me, he gave me a big hug, and he said, "You know what, Virginia? You need a guide dog." That's the first time I'd thought about a guide dog, back to that later. Let's go on with your questions.

## DOUG:

You've said that an important part of your Lighthouse program had to do with learning independent living skills. What kinds of things were involved in this aspect of your vocational rehabilitation?

## VIRGINIA:

I'm going to ramble a bit here and get ahead of the story. As a starter, don't forget, Doug, that my husband, Bob, is a tenured full professor at Purdue, so even though we spend much of the summer and the holidays together here in Miami, I'm basically on my own the great majority of the time at our Miami condo. So you can imagine how important learning day-to-day independent living skills was to me—not only a real declaration of independence, but also a great boost to my self-esteem! It was pretty frightening, early on in Miami as I thought about the prospect of living as a totally blind person, to imagine not being able to take care of myself, so I soaked up every last bit of the practical guidance the Lighthouse offered, believe me, for getting through the day-to-day things at home. And, you know, even if Bob were with me at home all year, and he will be in just a few years, I'd want him to be my husband and occasional helpmate, but definitely not my full-time caregiver. So, anyway, let me tell you a few things about the skills and tools for getting through day-to-day living at home, keeping in mind that it's an ongoing learning and adapting process, and no amount of training at the Lighthouse could have prepared me for every possible situation.

Why don't I start with the kitchen? One of the first really useful things I learned at the Lighthouse in my independent living training was to wear oven gloves, which are a specialty item sold in our store here at the Lighthouse, so when I'm cooking I don't accidentally hit the side of the oven when I'm taking out a hot dish. Another simple but really important independent living trick-of-the-trade is to put a contrasting tray on the counter top so if you have a little vision you see the contrast. And if you've totally lost your vision, which is my situation now, I can work on the tray, and spills are easy to clean up by just rinsing the tray. To be completely honest, even though I'm an avid learner, I now and then ignore the tips I've been taught; of course, I can't hold the Lighthouse responsible for my occasional lapses of good behavior. So, when I make Bob a cup of coffee and accidentally spill some coffee on the counter as I fill the coffeemaker, it's disheartening—and a blow to my pride—to learn I've left some coffee grounds on the counter, even after wiping it off, because I didn't use the tray like I'd been taught. But I chide myself, "Virginia, you're incorrigible; why didn't you use the procedure you were taught and put the coffeemaker on the tray?"

Staying in the kitchen, how do you think I can tell different kinds of soup apart when I'm alone, since the cans are the same? Rubber bands are a quick solution. Rubber band one type if you buy only two kinds. And if you have many different types of soup, use a Braille labeler. This is just like a print label machine but the letters are Braille dots. So, I take a three by five note card, put a Braille label on the card and rubber band that around the soup can. There are new and fancier technologies that will help in the kitchen, such as bar code scanners and a cell phone that can take a picture of print material and through optical recognition software in the cell read the label on a can or box. But, often simple techniques found in every home like different paper clips and rubber bands work great. Bump dots are on my flat panel refrigerator water dispenser and microwave so that I just push on and off, set the minutes for the microwave, and select ice or water on the refrigerator. Also, the strips people put in bathtubs to avoid slipping can be cut small and also used for tactile recognition of items.

Now we come to clothes, which I get asked about all the time. At the Lighthouse, I learned about Braille labeling, and you can purchase Braille labels identifying various colors of clothing in the Lighthouse specialty store. Not always the most methodical person in the world where small details are concerned, I said to myself: "Forget spending all that time labeling, just have someone help you sort clothes: black on the left, brown on the right." Yes, black has an "l" in the word for "left" and brown has an "r" for "right." Well one day, after organizing my closet, I said to myself, "Why do all of my clothes follow that rule but my shoes are just the opposite? Oh, well, I'll just remember that shoes are the opposite." That works as long as you put things back immediately after wearing the items. One bad habit I have when I get home from work is immediately get out of my work clothes. I kick off my high heels and throw my suit jacket over the back of the sofa, and then in the bedroom day after day I take off my clothes and throw them over the back of the sofa. Now, it's the weekend and some items made by the same manufacturer feel the same and I say to myself, "Is this the black skirt or the white skirt?" And I think, "What did you wear all week?"

and I can't remember. Or, "Why did I buy these suits in three different colors with the same fabric?" Then I might just wait for someone to visit to get things back in order. One morning I even asked someone in the elevator at my condo if both items I was wearing were green. There's always the option of running back and changing into the right skirt.

Now, you'll recall that Bob is at Purdue teaching during the school year, but when he comes down for the summer and witnesses this disorganization, he's always pretty appalled. He's an engineer, after all, and they're naturally well-organized and neat, so he feels responsible for helping get things back in order on the clothes front. Once, for example, he bought clothespins and went through all of my high-heeled shoes. By the way, he's said over and over that I have way too many pairs of shoes and I shouldn't ever wear the two- to three-inch heels because I might trip and fall someday. My response to that is always, "But I immediately lose five pounds when I get two inches taller!" So anyway, Bob pairs up all of my shoes and rearranges the closet so the black pairs are on the left and the brown on the right, and he attaches every pair with a clothespin, with one pin style for black shoes, and the other for brown. Bob's very logical theory is that the differences between the clothespins will always tell me what side I should put my shoes on at the end of the day. Well, you can imagine his frustration when in a hurry getting home to get on the computer or answer the phone I just kick my shoes off, and, you know, we have to start all over. Well, my theory is that neatness is a grossly overrated virtue!

Just to mention a couple of little things, there's sewing on missing buttons, which really worried me when I arrived at the Lighthouse for my training. Well, the Lighthouse sells special needles in its shop with a tiny opening at the top. What you do is stab the needle into a bar of soap and then pull your thread tight, and with thread tight between both your hands, shove it onto the opening on the head of the needle. And what about ironing clothes? Do you know how I reach for a hot iron without getting burned? I simply run my fingers along the cord to the iron handle. Well, I could go on and on about the simple but extremely important tricks of the personal coping trade, but you've probably heard enough.

## DOUG:

That summer of 2001, you completed your vocational rehabilitation program at the Lighthouse, made the dramatic decision not to return to Purdue, and after you finished your guide dog training, began to divide your time between West Lafayette and Miami, eventually joining the Lighthouse Board of Directors. Tell me about that period.

## VIRGINIA:

Deciding to go to New York for guide dog training was a real milestone for me, but I was really skeptical when my instructor first broached the idea. You remember my walk alone to the park I told you about, when my instructor said I needed a guide dog? Well, I'm thinking, "A guide dog? I just got used to this cane, and I just made it to the park by myself, and I'm so happy, and now he's telling me, 'You'd be great with a guide dog.'" It was really a foreign idea. What came to my mind immediately was the blind people on the corner with guide dogs and tin cups in Chicago when I worked there on LaSalle Street as an investment analyst, and I said, "Gosh, I just got used to this cane, and now

I'm going to go stand on a street corner in Chicago with my guide dog and a tin cup." And my instructor said, "Oh, no. Those people are situationally blind." I said, "Situationally blind? What in heaven's name is that?" He said, "They're not really blind—just for the situation. You're not going to need a tin cup."

So I asked him what was involved in getting a guide dog, and he explained that I'd need to spend a month in New York, living at a guide dog school and learning everything I'd need to know to live and work with my guide dog. And he said, "I don't tell a lot of people that they'd be great with a guide dog, but you would. You're fit, and you'd be able to take care of a dog." Well, that would mean a total of four months away from Purdue, and I said to myself, "I'll bet any amount of money that Purdue isn't about to put up with a fourth month away. If I did manage to make it back, I definitely wouldn't have the same job." A light bulb went off in my head. I never discussed with Bob that I wasn't going back to Purdue. I just did it. I called the provost, and I said, "Hi, it's Virginia here. How are things going? I want to give you a month's notice. I need to spend more time learning how to be a successful blind person, and so I won't be coming back at the end of my three month leave." Then I delivered the same message to the president, and that was formally the end of the Purdue phase of my journey; I never went back and I never second guessed the decision. To my way of thinking, I didn't really have a choice, since I realized that if I really wanted to function at a high level I needed a guide dog. I couldn't stand the thought of shortchanging myself by not taking advantage of every opportunity I had.

**DOUG:**

Why don't you tell us about your guide dog training before we go on?

**VIRGINIA:**

To begin with, up to then I'd been anything but a dog person, and now I was going away for a month to a guide dog school to learn how to use a dog. The first day at the school, Guiding Eyes for the Blind in New York, they told us to put away our white canes, which I'd just a few months ago learned to use and had gotten comfortable with. They were getting us ready for our dog, which meant checking our walking pace, our gait, our build, our strength. They gave me the biggest dog in the class, named Tracker. I'll never forget meeting Tracker; they brought the new dog to your room and you were supposed to play with the dog for an hour to start the really important bonding process. Not being used to dogs, I wasn't sure how to play with a dog so I sat on the floor and just let him lick my face. Little did I know then what a wonderful journey Tracker and I would make together, including his witnessing me fall into Biscayne Bay from the sea wall outside my condo. I'll tell you about that, even though I'm getting a little ahead of the story.

One Saturday, when I was back at my condo in Miami, Tracker and I were walking along my condo property looking onto Biscayne Bay. You know, your guide dog is trained to lead you when the harness is on. I was just bending over to put the harness on Tracker when, unknown to me, as I found out later from a security guard, a nanny came along with a baby buggy and cut between Tracker and the grass where he was finishing doing his thing. When I bent over to put the harness on, Tracker stepped to the side to let the nanny and buggy pass between the grass and him; this meant I also stepped to the right and immediately realized my right foot was not on the ground but, like in slow motion, I was on my way into the Bay. I'd never seen Biscayne Bay, of course, and naturally I never thought about whether the tide was out or in. That's wasn't a small thing, since at low tide the drop would have been about twenty feet—onto cement-like sand and rock.

So I told myself to let go of Tracker, since it'd be tremendously difficult to get him out of the Bay on a ladder, and I resigned myself to having a swim, just like in a pool. Indeed, the tide was in and the water was deep, so it really was like falling into a swimming pool. When I came up, a gentleman who was standing on the sea wall looking down at me yelled, "Virginia, I'm a friend of your husband's. How can I help?" By the way, I was a little embarrassed since I was sure he'd heard the expletive that popped out of my mouth when I got my breath—understandable, but not my normal style. Bobbing in the water, I looked up and said calmly, "Oh, why don't we get a ladder so I can climb back up." That's what he did, and I climbed back up to the sea wall, to the applause of a crowd of onlookers that'd gathered for the unplanned entertainment. What a sight I must have been! Someone was nice enough to walk with me and Tracker back to my apartment. Tracker had just stayed on the edge watching the show, by the way. I thought to myself, "Virginia you've got to change your clothes pronto and get back out there and walk around." And that's exactly what I did. You see, Doug, for one thing I didn't want to get scared and lose my confidence. And I wanted people to see I was all right and not to worry.

Since we're on the subject of guide dogs, let me tell you about the transition from my original dog, Tracker, who I'd gotten in 2001, and the guide dog I now have, Gibney. In 2008, I began to notice that Tracker frequently just stared at me when I'd say "let's go," and when I walked him he didn't seem to be concentrating, and he was walking really slowly. Sometimes I felt like I was leading him and this could get me in trouble, so I asked Guiding Eyes to send a trainer to Miami to see what I was doing wrong. We walked together a few blocks in busy traffic near the Miami Lighthouse to a nearby restaurant, and after lunch the trainer said: "Virginia you need to put your name in for a new guide dog." This was unexpected, I thought that maybe I was not praising Tracker enough. You know, Tracker wasn't only a really wonderful companion, he'd also become a celebrity in Miami. He went everywhere with me, including the dance floor at our 75th Gala at the Biltmore. But the trainer told me that, just like people who sometimes need to retire, Tracker was done with working. I can't tell you what a blow this was, but I had to go on.

Tracker was part of my journey when I began to live as a totally blind person and when I began as the first blind CEO of the Miami Lighthouse, and now it would soon be time to say good-bye. I could not conceive of Tracker going back to the guide dog school, where someone would adopt him. What if they kept him on a chain outside or mistreated him in some other way? I couldn't stand the thought. So once again Bob came to the rescue, along with my daughter in Indianapolis. When Bob went back to Indiana after a holiday visit, he took Tracker with him and shares him with our daughter's family. I had to wait a few weeks before being introduced to my new guide dog, Gibney, who hit the ground running. He didn't have a problem finding an open doorway, getting me on an elevator, that kind of thing, but he's had to learn to deal with all the photos when we go to events together. Tracker was a natural who really did seem to pose for a photo, but at first Gibney would turn his hind side to the camera and just stare at me. But he's gradually becoming a networker like Tracker was and almost smiles for the camera now.

OK, let's get back to 2001. Later that summer, when I got my guide dog, Tracker, and graduated from the training program in New York, I was told that I needed to stay in one place with my new canine companion for a full two months. Now I was confronted with another turning-point decision: Would I bring my new guide dog back to Miami or to our home in West Lafayette, where Bob would be returning for the fall semester at Purdue? So I thought about this, and I said to Bob, "You know what? I'm inclined to go back to Miami because if I need any help with mobility there's always the Lighthouse. Plus I've really fallen in love with the Lighthouse—what it does, the people I know there. What do you think?" He agreed that it made sense for me to stay in our condo in Miami, while he returned to Purdue to teach his fall classes. So in late June, I began working with my new guide dog in Miami, and Bob returned to Purdue on August 1. That's when I began to get heavily involved as a volunteer at the Lighthouse.

Here I was, down here in Miami alone after Bob left, and, since I really wanted to be busy doing something worthwhile, I went to the Lighthouse and said to the people there, "If you need speakers about the Lighthouse or speakers about guide dogs, I'd love to be able to do that." So they said "Great," and began to send me out to various schools and service organizations, where I talked about what the Lighthouse was all about and the important services it was providing in Greater Miami. This pretty visible work brought me to the attention of the Lighthouse leadership in a different way, was kind of like an entrée to the professional side of things there. I also started a dog guide group at the Lighthouse. There aren't a lot of guide dog users in Miami, but we'd meet at the Lighthouse. Stuff like that. You're probably curious about what I said about Miami not having many guide dog users, but it was true then and still is. You know, in order to get a guide dog you've got to be able to walk a mile in the morning and a mile in the afternoon at the guide dog school. You've got to be healthy. You can't have heart disease. You can't have arthritis. You've got to be pretty competent. You've got to have very good orientation and mobility skills. There are certainly guide dog users, but many, many more cane users.

Now two months went by, and I could travel, so I went back to Indiana to be with Bob, which was the natural thing to do, but I was a little worried. Since I wasn't any longer at Purdue, I wasn't sure what I was going to do to keep busy. This is the first time in years that I didn't have anything in particular to do, and I hadn't plotted anything out. I might have mentioned earlier that our house was way out in the country, so it wasn't obvious how to keep busy. I say, okay, I'm going to go to the gym. I'm going to be really fit. So every day I hire a taxi to take me to the gym. I work out, and then I go home, and then I listen to books on tape. I probably became one of the most fit and well-read people around! But when you listen to books on tape you tend to fall asleep, at least I did, and I'd never been the kind of person that falls asleep in the afternoon. Then my husband and my kids would notice, it's three o'clock in the afternoon, and Mom's sleeping. And Bob told me later that he'd come home with me because he was worried since this definitely wasn't the Virginia he knew. My kids said to me, "Did you fall asleep because you were feeling exhausted?" I said, "No, I'm sleeping because my life now isn't very demanding or exciting: maybe going to the gym in the morning; maybe having lunch with a few people; walking the dog out on a country road; listening to books on tape." That was my life. Later on I knew that that really bothered my husband.

Well, being home definitely wasn't going to work, for me or Bob. He was happily occupied doing research and teaching at Purdue, while I was dozing off in the afternoon listening to a book, having an occasional lunch to look forward to, along with my workouts and walking Tracker. No way that could continue without me going bonkers! So I was home only a few months, when I began to go back and forth between West Lafayette and Miami, and it wasn't long before I was spending the great majority of my time at our Miami condo, and most of that time I spent at the Lighthouse, or out in the community representing the Lighthouse. Sure, I missed Bob, but I was busy, I was happy, I was managing to live on my own. But I still didn't have a clue what I was meant to be and do, beyond volunteering. I certainly wasn't thinking about becoming a member of the Lighthouse Board of Directors, so the invitation caught me by surprise.

## DOUG:

So tell me about the next phase of the journey, when you became a Lighthouse Board member, and eventually interim and then permanent president and CEO.

## VIRGINIA:

What you've got to understand, Doug, is that I didn't plot out any kind of career path at the Lighthouse early-on. I never said to myself, "OK, you're here now, how do you get ahead, become a board member, maybe get an administrator job? What's the first step, what do you do next . . . ?" All I knew in the fall of 2001 was that I loved living in Miami and being at the Lighthouse, and the more I knew about what the Lighthouse did in the community and the better I got to know both the staff and the clients, the more I wanted to be around them. It was natural to begin speaking and volunteering in other ways. I was using professional skills, and I didn't need authority or money to be satisfied. You know that I'm a really ambitious person, so you might be skeptical about what I've just said, but I can only tell you that's the way it was. What eventually transpired was maybe destined to happen, but not because I consciously plotted it out. To my mind, I was there, I was able, and when opportunities came, I was willing.

Now, I don't mean to say that I never thought about possibilities now and then, just that there wasn't any kind of grand strategy. Because there were times, while I was going through the vocational rehabilitation program, when I would say to myself, "You know, if I was running the Lighthouse, I would do this differently. I would get more grants. I would have a music program." Because of my experience at Purdue, things were always coming into my mind. I'd ask myself things like, "Why don't they have speakers in here during lunch hour? Why can't they have a big music program? Blind people would love music." You know, I'd have these ideas. I wondered why the powers-that-be didn't treat the Lighthouse like a university, write grant proposals, those kinds of things. After all, they had educational programs, teachers, and students, so the university model really did fit, at least generally.

One afternoon—this would have been the summer of 2001—I was walking with one of my mobility teachers, when he asked me if I'd heard that the Lighthouse CEO, who'd been at the helm for twenty-four years, was retiring. Well, that got me to thinking—thinking, mind you, not strategizing—and I got in touch with one of my counselors. I thought, "OK, they're supposed to be rehabilitating me for a new vo-cation, and I'm supposed to have a career goal, so why shouldn't it be CEO of the Lighthouse?" So the counselor and I are strolling around outside the Lighthouse; I remember it like yesterday. I'm walking with my cane, and I'm so proud that I'm walking as fast as she is. By the way, I'd started walking by myself to the metro, to Walgreens—things that were really significant emotional events to me since I never thought I'd be doing them again. Anyway, while we were walking around, I told her that I'd learned that the Lighthouse CEO was planning to retire, and I said that I wanted to put my hat in the ring for the position. I'll never forget what she said: "Oh, Virginia, that board would never pick a blind person to be the CEO of the Lighthouse." And I said, "Oh, I know someone on the board who's blind," and she just said, "You're wasting your time. They'd never pick you."

Well that was the end of that. I didn't put my name in, and maybe they wouldn't have considered me seriously for the job, but I'll never know, will I? I got an early lesson about low expectations for peo-ple who are blind or visually impaired. I honestly did feel it wasn't far-fetched to think of myself as a serious candidate, even if I hadn't up to then thought much about it, or made being CEO a formal goal, you know, part of a career plan. Well, to me, once I did start thinking about it, there was a fit, and it wasn't a stretch to see it.

The CEO who was retiring had served the agency well over the years, as far as I could tell; he was a dedicated guy and apparently pretty widely respected and admired, but he was a traditional social-service leader—a social worker, a vision-rehabilitation person. He wasn't a businessman, and he wasn't really into growing and diversifying the Lighthouse as a kind of social enterprise. That's where I came in, with my background at Purdue. I couldn't help but see the potential for building the Lighthouse into a larger, stronger institution, given the experience I'd had at Purdue. Even in my earliest time as a student there, I'd see things and say to myself, "Gee, what about that, couldn't we do it differently? Or why aren't we doing this, couldn't we get it started?" So when I got the word that the position was open, I thought, "You know what? You've got the skills. There's no difference between a Purdue University and a Miami Lighthouse. They need their donations. They've got the students. It's just a different approach." Believe it or not, the Lighthouse had only one grant then, as far as I can recall. They got a grant to start the Blind Babies Program. They weren't thinking about the need to get new revenues flowing in, to fund new programs, by going out and getting more grants. They just didn't think much about it. The attitude was, "Whatever money the government gives us, that's the money we're going to live on." And I thought to myself, "You know, if you were to write grant proposals they could do so much more."

I wasn't thinking of it in terms of "I want to be a CEO." I was thinking in terms of, "In order to do what they need to do, you are the kind of person that can do that, but that requires being the CEO." Do you know what I'm saying? And given what the job required, I think with my experience I could do it pretty well. But those were just thoughts that I had. And then when someone squelched it, I backed off and thought, "Oh, well. I guess not." But it was a mistake. I should have put my name in, only because then there would have been earlier recognition of me as a potential leader down the road. Who knows? But, you know, maybe there's a plan. Maybe. I mean there might be a plan for all of us. Was it God's will that I went blind? Was it God's will? I don't know. Is there a plan? I don't know, but maybe there is. So I wasn't meant to be CEO then, wasn't really ready, and when the opportunity came again, I was. Who knows?

Anyway, that was in the summer of 2001, and after my guide dog training and two months back in Miami with Tracker, I was alternating between West Lafayette with Bob and the condo in Miami, where I was eventually spending the great majority of my time, and when I was in Miami, I was almost always either at the Lighthouse, at meetings of the guide dog group I'd organized or of the Miami Chapter of the American Council of the Blind, or I'd be out in the community talking about the Lighthouse. It'd become my passion, and I loved being there. But I was still completely surprised when I got the call, in early 2004, from the woman who'd become CEO in 2002, asking me if I'd be interested in becoming a member of the Lighthouse Board of Directors. I didn't have to mull it over at all. I just said, "Great, I'd be honored. Tell me when and where and I'll be there." If I recall correctly, I attended my first meeting as a Lighthouse Board member in September 2004, and later that fall I was elected treasurer of the Board.

I don't have much of a story to tell about the few Board meetings I attended before becoming interim CEO of the Lighthouse in February 2005. I felt pretty comfortable at Board meetings, since I'd served on nonprofit boards back in Indiana and, as you'll recall, I worked closely with the Purdue University Board of Trustees. By the time I got on the Board, I could use JAWS to read the floppy disks containing Board meeting materials that arrived before meetings. Becoming treasurer wasn't much of a stretch since people knew about my financial experience at Purdue, and I was pretty vocal in meetings of the Board's finance committee, which I'd been assigned to. Being asked to serve as treasurer had given me some pause, since it seemed like a pretty big leap for someone who'd been a vocational rehabilitation student only a little over three years earlier and hadn't even been on the Board for six months, but I figured my experience at Purdue would stand me in good stead. What worried me most was the demand on my time; taking this job on would mean being virtually full time in Miami, while Bob would be holding the fort truly alone back in West Lafayette. But when I asked for Bob's advice, he was his usual cheerleader self. "Do you really want to do it?" he asked me when I told him I'd been offered the position, and when I said I did, he just said, "Well, life is short; go for it!" What would I ever have done without Bob? You know, I did—and do—really care about my marriage, and just imagine how much tension there'd have been in my life during this time if Bob hadn't been so encouraging. I've really lucked out in so many ways, but at the top of the list of blessings is Bob.

Now, what I didn't expect when I took over the treasurer position is that I'd end up having to sign every check that the Lighthouse issued. At first, I wasn't sure how I, as the new—blind!—treasurer, could handle such a sensitive responsibility, but I pretty quickly came up with a solution. I'd have the Lighthouse chief financial officer send me an electronic check register, with the beginning balance and all the checks laid out, and I wouldn't sign any check that wasn't on the register unless the CFO could explain it to my satisfaction. It worked, I'm happy to say, and serving successfully as treasurer is certainly the main reason why I was asked to become interim CEO of the Lighthouse in early February 2005, when the CEO unexpectedly resigned. Another thing in my favor was my major budgeting experience at Purdue, since when I got on the Board, I learned that the Lighthouse didn't, at least that year, have a formal, written budget, which the Board really needed to stay on top of things, financially speaking. It's amazing, in retrospect, what a good job the Board did in overseeing performance even without a budget, but it was a challenge.

By this time, I felt pretty sure I was up to the challenge of running the organization, but, you know, I wasn't expecting to hold the job permanently; I figured it might last a week, a month, who knew? In my mind, filling in when the Lighthouse seriously needed me was a way of paying them back for the great things they'd done for me. In the same spirit, I insisted that I do the job without pay—pro bono, as they say. After all, my vocational rehabilitation training, which transformed my life, hadn't cost me a penny, and with my insurance and Social Security disability checks and Bob's salary, I wasn't pressured to earn money. It just seemed like the right thing to do at the time, and, in retrospect, I was right. It's funny as I think about it, since I guess I should have worried that some people might take me less seriously if I was working for free, but that never even occurred to me back then.

So there I am in February 2005, at the helm of the Lighthouse, while the Board launched a national search for a permanent CEO. One of my senior executives threw her hat in the ring, but I wasn't asked to apply, and I didn't. In fact, now that I wasn't on the Board any longer, I was really outside the loop—didn't know anything about the search process. In the back of my mind, I figured there was a possibility they'd ask me to apply at some point, if they decided they wanted someone with high-level management and business experience, but I knew that I didn't bring any of the programming experience they might decide they needed, so I might end up not making the list at all. But that didn't bother me, since I was playing it completely by ear, without any expectations about the future. That said, I don't want to give the impression that I saw being the interim top guy as some kind of holding action, like I'm just warming the seat for the eventual "real" CEO. I intended to get some serious stuff done as long as I was sitting in the CEO seat, and budget was at the top of the list.

You'll recall me saying that the Lighthouse didn't have a formal budget that year. I know that's hard to believe, but it's true, so my first week on the job I pulled my senior managers together and told them that we would meet as often as we needed to in order to get a full-fledged revenue and expenditure budget together for the March 2005 Board meeting, only a month away, and we got it done. Thank heaven for my Purdue experience; I knew budgeting inside out, so I could lead the process of developing the Lighthouse budget knowing precisely what we needed to do. I also did some reaching out in the community to other nonprofit CEOs who could give me insights about being a successful nonprofit CEO, especially the potholes that I could stumble into unawares. For example, visiting with the CEO of

Goodwill, I asked him: "If you were to give me a piece of advice for succeeding early on, what would that be?" What he told me proved to be invaluable, especially when I got the permanent appointment in June: "Spend your time in-house. Don't travel out of town. Don't visit other places or attend national meetings. You need to stay home and focus on internal operations. If you do that for a year, and things are humming along, then you can begin to make forays into the wider world. But only when the house is in order." The other really valuable piece of advice he gave me was to stay close to my Board, treating them as my top-tier CEO customer and my primary constituent. I knew this from my Purdue days, but I needed to hear it again.

Coming to the Board with a complete, carefully prepared budget in March made a real impression, which is probably the main reason I was asked in May 2005 to pull my resume together and become a candidate for the permanent position. Well, you know the outcome. After the Board meeting announcing that I'm the permanent CEO, I got back to my office to find that one of my most senior and key executives, who'd been in the running for the job, had left her office keys on my desk and walked out. What a welcome!

### DOUG:

You've been permanent CEO of the Miami Lighthouse now for a little over three years. Most readers can probably pretty easily picture you playing your internal operational role, using JAWS to read email and reports, chairing meetings, attending committee and full Board meetings, and the like. But I imagine that one of the most challenging facets of your work, as a blind CEO, is getting out in the community, playing your ambassadorial and advocacy roles. Would you share some of your experiences in this regard?

## VIRGINIA:

I knew from the get-go that it was really important for me to get out into the community—to Chamber of Commerce and Rotary Club meetings, anytime that there was another nonprofit honoring someone at a gala or a special event. Don't forget, I'd gotten involved in getting grants at Purdue, and I didn't have any question that as the new CEO of the Lighthouse I'd need to be out there, rubbing elbows with other leaders and being recognized by philanthropists. But walking into a room full of people is one thing if you're sighted, and you can very quickly scan the room and position yourself where you want to be. But I'd walk into a room not even able to read someone's name tag much less see across the room to decide which table I should pick to sit at. So I pretty quickly learned some strategies. For example, there'd be times that it would be appropriate to ask another colleague at work to join me, but in other situations it was more appropriate that I went by myself. And so in those cases it would require calling some other CEO, or a board member of another organization, thinking of who would be there that I knew, calling them ahead of time and saying, "I'm going to be going to the Red Cross luncheon today where you're honoring so-and-so, and when I get there do you mind looking for me so that I can sit with you?" And that strategy has worked pretty well, but I've had some scary moments.

For example, very recently I needed to go to an event, and I was going to go with my development officer, but she was ill, so I said to myself, "You've still got to go, Virginia, it's in the job description." In this case, there were two philanthropists I wanted to connect with. One had been very good to me, and another's family foundation was giving us money, so there was a lot of opportunity there, and it was important to go. Well, I had someone drop me off at the hotel, and when I get inside the hotel, you know it's so important to smile and to say to the valet or whomever, "Oh, could you walk me to the elevator? Could you please push the up button?" And when I get in the elevator, "Would you please push nine for me?" Whenever I get off an elevator, my dog's going to head toward any voices he hears, and that worked beautifully that evening. I heard the voices, and I'm standing there and the first person to come up to me is this female philanthropist who says, "Virginia! I want my husband to meet you. I'm so glad you're here." And I said, "Well, I knew that you were being honored, and I really wanted to meet you." And I said to myself, "Virginia, that's why you dug down deep to get the courage, and you didn't say, 'Oh, well. I won't be able to go because my development person can't go with me.' " And so I was pretty proud of myself.

After the dinner was over I needed to use my cell phone to call the driver to tell him I was ready to be picked up, and when I and the two people I'd sat with stood up, they said they had to leave for another engagement and asked if I'd be all right alone. I said, "Oh, fine. No worry. My dog will find the door, and I'll just wait up here for my driver." So they weren't able to walk me out to the anteroom where the cocktail reception had been held, and I said to myself, "Don't worry. Tell your dog 'forward,' he'll find the doorway, and you'll just stand in the area where the cocktail party was." As I walked through the doorway one of the hostesses said, "Oh, Virginia. Do you need any help downstairs?" And I said, "Oh no. I'm going to stand up here and wait for my driver." And she said, "Well, you really should stand over here because we don't want you to block the doorway where everyone's coming out." I said, "Where is here?" And she said, "Oh, just go forward about ten feet and then just stand there." Well, the strategy of standing there turned out really well because up walked the very well-known philanthropist who'd been honored at the dinner and who I'd hoped to see, along with his wife. By the way, they'd made a ten-year pledge to the Lighthouse. When they greeted me, I said, "Oh, Paul, I'm so glad to see you. Congratulations for your award." "Virginia, we didn't know you were here. It really means a lot to us that you'd come by yourself."

So there I am, getting really animated, and I'm not holding my dog's harness. Now, when you hold the dog's harness, the dog knows he's in charge, and he's going to protect you. But I'm only holding his leash, and when you hold the leash he's no different from any pet. So I'm all caught up in the conversation, and I put my right hand out and feel something rubber. Seeing me do that, the people I was talking with said, "Hey, Virginia, do you know that you're standing right by the top of the escalator?" I said, "No, I had no idea." You know, with new technology escalators are very quiet, and I didn't have a clue where I was. Normally when you get off the escalator there's a metal walkway before you hit the carpet, but in this case the carpet went right up to where the rubber hand railing of the escalator was. Anyway, I said, "Help me move over." On the way home I was thinking to myself, "You know, you were probably one inch from disaster, all you had to do was step backwards, and that wouldn't have been pretty." Whenever I go out by myself, it's a wonderful feeling when I get in my door and say, "Wow, I was able to see those individuals I wanted to see, and I'm home safely." And I'm always a little bit proud that I've been able to get past the trepidation I'm normally feeling when I set out on my own.

Let me tell you about another experience I had, venturing out in the Miami community. It wasn't long after getting my new guide dog, Gibney, and the local Humane Society was having a fashion show. Not only does the Humane Society do really important work, it's also got a lot of great donors, so it's on my list of important stakeholders. Now, a few months earlier, I'd told the fellow who was putting on the fashion show for the Society that I was interested in participating, but he'd said, "Oh, Virginia, that would be so hard for you being blind. I just don't think you could do it." Anyway, not long before the show was to take place, I went to a luncheon, where I was chatting with the CEO of the Humane Society, and she was talking about the fashion show and how they were looking for people in the community with dogs. So I told her I'd love to be in the show. It struck me as a great way to get publicity for the Lighthouse, for people with guide dogs, and generally for people who are blind. She couldn't have been more positive, telling me, "What a great idea, having a guide dog. You're in the fashion show. I'll put you right behind Donna Shalala." You probably know that Donna is president of the University of Miami.

Without a lot of thought, I'd gotten myself into a pretty tough situation: parading in front of a thousand people on a forty-foot-long runway not much wider than a yard stick, along with several other participants with their dogs. And me with my new guide dog! I did have some second thoughts since something could pretty easily go wrong, but I thought it was worth the risk. So I got there early, kind of felt the steps and all that, and I said to myself, "If you fall off that stage you are going to be in big trouble." So I asked the people in charge if I could do a trial run with Gibney, since this was a new experience for both of us, and getting the go-ahead, I walked up the steps and started down the runway with my dog, who was walking on my left, which is where a guide dog's supposed to be. When I got to the end of the runway, I was told that I had to take the turn so I was on the outside— that way, the photographers could get my photo. I knew that if I was on the outside taking the turn and stepped a little too wide, I'd end up in the audience, so I insisted that the photographers would just have to figure out how to take the photo with me on the inside, and that's what we did.

Okay, so now it's the style show, and participants are lined up with their dogs, waiting their turn. Donna Shalala goes ahead of me down the runway, and I walk up the steps, and I stand there for a minute, thinking "You must be crazy, Virginia," and I tell my dog, "forward." I'd already counted that I had something like eighty steps to walk, so when we got to eighty, I told Gibney to turn, and as I made the turn, Doug, I was so thrilled that I hadn't stepped off the stage that I raised my hand and gave the audience a big smile and a wave, and I got a standing ovation. That Sunday morning, there we were—my dog and I—on the front page of the newspaper, so the Miami Lighthouse got some great publicity, and I proved to myself, once again, that I could get out there and do it, even if people told me I couldn't.

Dinners out can be a real challenge, by the way. For one thing, you don't always know what's in the plate someone's set down at your place. My husband once asked me, "How come when you have your fork in your hand sometimes it looks like you're stirring things around on your plate?" And I said, "Because I'm trying to figure out what's on my plate." When I can order the meal, I always pick food that's easy to eat, rather than what I might really be in the mood for. For example, mashed potatoes, French fries, lamb chops with a bone to pick up, and salads only when they can be chopped really small. But I usually don't eat a lot when I'm out in public. Imagine being blind and having a plate full of noodles. That would be very difficult to eat very gracefully!

But it's not just the food that causes problems. More than once here in Miami I've had trouble being seated at a restaurant with my guide dog, even though it's federal law that a blind person with a guide dog must be seated. It's not uncommon, in my experience, for the host or hostess just to be aware that dogs generally can't be brought into a restaurant by local health department regulations. Let me tell you about a fairly recent experience that gave me an opportunity to put on my advocacy hat. I was shopping in a very upscale department store with a former board member—we were looking for a gift for the outgoing board chair—and we decided to stop for lunch at the really nice restaurant in the store. When we walked up to the hostess, she said, "Oh, I'm sorry, but dogs are not allowed." And, by the way, this store was officially pet friendly, but they obviously didn't allow pets in their dining room. So this woman says, "I'm sorry, but you're not going to be able to eat here with your dog." And I said, "My dog is a guide dog. I'm blind." And she said, "It doesn't matter, you can't eat here." Now, we're trained to say, "Do we need the police department to explain the law to you?" but you hate to do that kind of thing. So my rule is, if they don't want you in the restaurant don't eat there because they're probably going to spit in your food in the food preparation area or something. You never know. So just don't eat there.

But anyway, I was in a situation where I needed to be there so I said, "If you can't seat us we'll probably just have to seat ourselves." So we went and seated ourselves, and it wasn't a real busy day so the chef came out, the hostess came out, and they kind of looked at us, and I kept talking and being very gracious, pretending everything was just fine. And now the employees are probably thinking, "Can you imagine? We told her not to bring that dog in here, and she still brought that dog in here? Who does she think she is?" I just ignored them, and when lunch was over and I said good-bye to my colleague, I went down to the store's business office and asked for the store manager, who when I'd told my story said, "Here's a coupon for a free meal, we hope you come back again." I said, "It's not that I need a free lunch. Imagine if you're on a date and you're blind. I'm an old horse, but what if you're young, impressionable, embarrassed—that person could be so humiliated." And I said, "So what you really need to do is put on a training program, because clearly you don't have a training program regarding the ADA." And, believe it or not, the manager just blew me off, saying, "What do you want me to do? I gave you a free lunch coupon."

Well, I decided to call the chain's president at the corporate headquarters, but when I was discussing this with my son, who had experience in retailing, he said, "Mom, they're just going to pass you off to the lawyers because they don't want to deal with it, and they're paying lawyers to handle these kinds of things, so don't say anything that sounds like you're going to be litigious. Instead tell them that this is a public relations issue—that they need to put on training so they don't get caught with a serious image problem. Then they'll listen." And so, lo and behold, when I called headquarters, I couldn't get through to the president but I was able to speak to his administrative assistant, and the first thing out of her mouth was, "Well, we don't deal with that. You'll have to take it up with our attorneys, who deal with this kind of complaint." And I had to say to her, "Oh, no, this isn't that I want to be litigious, I just want you to set up a training program, and I want to know when the training is conducted, and then this won't become a public relations issue." And my son was spot on. Because she said, "Oh, well, can I get back with you?" And at the end of the day I got a phone call from the president of this really prestigious chain's South Florida region, "I want you to know that today we conducted training for all of our staff regarding the ADA law." I said, "Well, thank you very much. That is what I needed to hear, and I appreciate that."

## DOUG:

Serving as an advocate for the blind and visually impaired is obviously a critical facet of your role as CEO of the Miami Lighthouse. I'd appreciate your saying more about this dimension of your CEO-ship.

## VIRGINIA:

I have to be an advocate for blind and visually impaired people because they're so often misunderstood, and people typically in my experience have such low expectations for them. For me, one of the saddest situations I see is a blind person who's got tremendous talent, or extraordinary intelligence, but because they're blind, their talent or intelligence is discounted. I detest low expectations based on the fact that a person has vision problems! Let me tell you a true story to make the point—about an assistant music instructor at the Lighthouse. This fellow has perfect pitch; you can touch a number on the cell phone, and he'll tell you what number you just pushed, because, you know, each number on the keypad has a different tone. Anyway, this really talented blind musician in his early twenties enrolled in the Lighthouse's vocational rehabilitation program. He could play the piano beautifully by ear, and I had great expectations for him. So one day I went up to our music production studio, and he wasn't there. When I asked where he was, I was told he'd gotten a job. "Really," I said, "What kind of job?" I was told that he'd been placed in a clerical position. "Office clerical work?" I said. "Come on now. What sense does that make when he's so incredibly talented in music?"

To make a long story short, we were able to bring this young fellow on board at the Lighthouse as an assistant music instructor. I have to tell you, this young man progressed so beautifully, and he was a tremendous help with the new students in our music production program. I had to create a job on the spot, even though we didn't really have a vacancy, because it just would have broken my heart to see such a talented young man spending his time on mundane clerical tasks. By the way, I think he's now interviewing for a pretty well-paying job as a church pianist, which pleases me to no end.

There's another aspect to advocacy: teaching and encouraging blind people to advocate for themselves, and that includes kids, not just adults. The Miami Lighthouse isn't part of the public school system here in Miami, but blind and visually impaired students do come here in the summers and on Saturdays and holidays. I have a great story about one of our Lighthouse participants, a ten-year-old, who made us tremendously proud when he stood up for himself. Let me give you a little background. With the shortage of funding in the Miami Public Schools, blind kids have a tough time getting what they need because of the low incidence of blindness. For example, if a student blind from birth is to succeed in school, she needs a Braille note taker, like the one you've seen me use in meetings. But unlike mine, it has Braille cells on it, rather than the normal typewriter keypad, and a blind kid needs to learn how to use it really early in school so he can keep up in class. But that piece of equipment costs around $5,000, and it wasn't being provided to blind kids in the Miami Schools.

To get to the story, I recently hosted the Dade County state legislative delegation over lunch at the Lighthouse, and this ten-year-old boy sang "Proud To Be an American" for the group It was so sweet. Afterward, one of the legislators went up and started talking with him. I was standing nearby, and I heard the little fellow say, out of the clear blue sky, that he'd gotten all Fs in school because he didn't have the equipment he needed to succeed. "That's not right," I heard him tell the legislator, who was fascinated, "that I fail because my family can't afford to buy a note taker that the schools should be taking care of." To my surprise, the legislator told the boy that "you and I are going to see the superintendent of schools," and asked him, "Would you go with me to see him?" I'm not actually sure they ended up going together, but there's no question the legislator learned about a very important issue—and from a ten-year-old, too. That's advocacy!

I'll give you one more example, which actually goes back to when I was volunteering at the Miami Lighthouse before becoming its interim CEO and spending time in both West Lafayette and Miami. You probably know what an accessible pedestrian signal is. When you're standing at an intersection, you can hear it go "beep, beep, beep," and when you hit the button it'll say, "You're at the intersection of Eighth Avenue and Seventh Street. Okay to cross." Well, back in 2004, if I recall correctly, there was only one such signal in Miami, and we obviously could use accessible signals near the Lighthouse. I'd heard a lecture about the signals at a meeting of the American Council for the Blind that was held at the Lighthouse. So, now that I'm back in West Lafayette trying to figure out what my life's going to be—and remember, I told you I would go to the gym almost every day. I wanted to be able to walk to my husband's office, which was only a block away, rather than going back home after working out. But you had to cross a big intersection, and it was impossible for me with my dog. It was a big, rounding corner so you couldn't line yourself up square at the intersection, and it was a five-way intersection with cars coming and going every which way. And these cars could make a right-hand turn right on into traffic anytime. That intersection was anything but accessible, right?

It really got to me, and I said to myself, "I know that there're probably twenty other visually impaired people on this campus who're having trouble at this terrible intersection." So I called a couple of them, and they said, "Yeah. We can't even go over to Lambert Field House." That's where the football stadium and basketball arena are, and where they have yoga classes and stuff like that. And so I started to make a few phone calls to local and state offices, and I was getting the run-around; I think they figured I was just being difficult, you know, a pest. So I asked my husband, Bob, who's a civil engineer, if he'd mind if I called the head of the Indiana Department of Transportation and told him that my husband was a civil engineering professor at Purdue. By the way, the engineering department at Purdue is the research arm for the Department of Transportation. So that's what I did. I was then back in my condo in Miami, and Bob, who was on break, was sitting in on the call. So when I reach the head of the department, I tell him that Bob's a professor of civil engineering at Purdue, and I explain the accessible signal issue. I then said, "Wouldn't it be great if there was a small grant to study this? And I'm certain that my husband would be very willing to take this on." This guy now knows that I'm really serious, and he says, "Let me get back to you. I need to talk to the head of the research section." Do you know that my husband got a $30,000 grant to study the intersection and to become one of Indiana's experts on accessible pedestrian signals? He even went to Indianapolis and helped testify for some people in Indianapolis. This is because I said to the head of the Department of Transportation, "It's my civil right, and every other blind person's civil right to be able to walk down the street. And why are there certain Purdue students who, because they're visually impaired, can't go to a certain part of Purdue's campus?" And you know what? There's now an accessible pedestrian signal there, and people really appreciate it. Because you've got an armful of groceries. You're pulling your computer. You're busy, and people are crossing all different ways, and it's dangerous. But now people know they can stand here and chitchat until they hear it say, "Okay to cross."

So now I'm interim CEO of the Lighthouse, and I'm thinking, "Okay, I originally heard about accessible signals at the Lighthouse, and there's only one accessible signal I know of in the city. I'm going to do the same thing here in Miami right by the Lighthouse. It'll be a great training tool for the Lighthouse Orientation and Mobility Program." And so one break when Bob was here in Miami I start making some phone calls, and I'm getting the same run-around I'd gotten back in Indiana. You know, this is under the state, that's under the city of Miami, that kind of thing—pointing the finger. So, I say, "We need to get everyone together and have a meeting." And the meeting takes place in my conference room at the Lighthouse, with state and county traffic people and the head of ADA for Miami-Dade County, who happens to be in a wheelchair. I had my husband, Bob, at the meeting, too, and he's written a publication on this, a publication that's used in Washington, D.C., about accessible pedestrian signals. And so, guess what? Now there are more accessible pedestrian signals in Miami, including near the Lighthouse, and also in Indiana.

## DOUG:

I'm aware that you've been a frequent visitor to the Florida state capitol in Tallahassee, wearing your advocate hat. Tell me about what it's like traveling by plane.

## VIRGINIA:

This past legislative session in Tallahassee I went three times by myself. Let me walk you through that. When I take a plane somewhere, I memorize my ticket confirmation number, and I make sure I'm on a direct flight, which is pretty easy flying from Miami, since it's a major hub. My guide dog always sits at my feet in the cab, so we don't leave dog hair on the seat. I travel very lightly; pulling a suitcase doesn't work for me since I need both hands for handling my dog. One hand's to hold the harness and leash and the other in case I need to give the dog a correction—that is, a pull on the leash with my right hand, which tightens the collar and makes the dog get his focus back. I carry money in my pocket for tips and a shoulder duffle bag that has both dog food and clothing. I always make sure to wear lightweight, wrinkle-free suits. And mix and match. My colleagues will tell you I'm a living lesson and role model where packing light's concerned! I carry my bills specially folded so I know what I'm giving the taxi driver: for example, a twenty is folded first lengthwise, and then widthwise, into quarters.

When I get out of the taxi, I ask for special assistance after checking in curbside and getting my boarding pass. Then the person giving me special assistance walks me through security and to the gate. This is really important where security's concerned because I've learned that the security staff are often not well trained on guide dogs and might try to grab my leash and take my dog, ask me to take the dog harness off, etc. Taking a blind person's guide dog away is like taking a disabled person's wheelchair. The way it's supposed to work is I go through screening first, while my dog sits waiting—he's on a long leash—and then I say "come," and he goes through, setting off the alarm, of course, and then he's checked separately while I'm holding the leash. However, it's not uncommon for security staff not to know what to do when I arrive at the security checkpoint, which is really frustrating and aggravating. My first inclination when something like that happens is to get huffy and say something like, "You guys need some better training," you just so much want to put it in their face. It takes a lot of self-control to smile and be gracious because you really do need people's help—you do need friends—and alienating people just for emotional satisfaction doesn't make any sense. Anyway, you never really know who's observing you at security. There could always be one of your donors in line behind you, and so you want them to think, "She was really gracious even though security was totally clueless."

You've got to take a small commuter plane from Miami to Tallahassee, so we ride an airport bus from the gate to the plane. My guide dog's trained to walk up the bus steps, walk me down the steps to the tarmac, walk me up the airplane steps, and sit at my feet in the bulkhead section of the plane. Of course, before flying anywhere, I only give my dog a tiny amount of water that day and no solid food, and when I get off the flight I've got to find grass quickly. I can't really count on things ever going like clockwork, needless to say. For example, a few months ago—I'm deviating from my Tallahassee story for a minute—I was flying to Indianapolis and had to change planes in Charlotte (violating my direct flight rule). My flight from Charlotte was delayed because of some kind of mechanical problem. It was one of those really frustrating experiences that frequent flyers are all-too-familiar with. We boarded, sat on the runway for an hour, went back to the gate, deplaned, sat in the lobby for an hour, boarded a second time, and then deplaned again. That's the kind of situation that spells trouble when you're traveling with your guide dog!

But, as it often the case, I'd made a friend who came to my rescue; this time it was the pilot. The last time I'd deboarded, I make a point of saying to the pilot, as I walked by the cockpit on the way out, "This must be soooo frustrating for you." He walked out with me, and I mentioned that I was very worried about my dog since four hours had passed, and going back through security would be a real problem—he needed grass, and right away! The pilot, my new friend, said, "Look, let me do it for you; I can get through security pretty easy." In about fifteen minutes he returned Gibney to me, saying "Success, Virginia." Actually, when he returned the dog to me, we'd already reboarded, and he brought Gibney right to my seat. There's more to the story. The pilot hadn't put Gibney's choke collar back on correctly after going through security, and so it fell off and slid to the back of the plane. As we were taking off, I felt Gibney's neck, and the collar was missing. Almost in a panic, I asked the guy across the aisle if he'd seen the collar. Then I called the stewardess, who said, "Oh someone said they heard something sliding on the floor," and she found it. All's well that ends well, as they say. That was quite a trip, and it proved again that going out of my way to be nice and make friends pays off. And it's a much more pleasant way to pass time than constantly getting riled up and pushing people back. Now let's get back to that Tallahassee trip I was telling you about.

So when I arrived in Tallahassee on that commuter plane, I took a taxi to the hotel I always stay at because it has grass and I'm familiar with it. I've made an effort to get to know the hotel manager and the people at the main desk, so everyone is always very friendly and attentive when I'm staying there. I always ask for a room number ending 02 or 04 so that I know it is at the end of the hallway and not easy to miss. On the elevator I typically ask someone when I first get there if the floor is what I think it should be so as not to end up on the wrong floor. Then after getting freshened up I call a taxi to take me to our lobbyist's office, where I meet someone who'll escort me to the capitol to start the meetings they've set up for me.

On one of these trips to Tallahassee, when a senator involved in health and human services issues had called a special meeting, as we walked to the capitol a huge rainstorm broke loose, the rain blew in all directions, and we knew it was either miss the meeting or arrive soaking wet. I told the lobbyist I was walking with that we didn't have a choice; the meeting was too important to miss. So we were dripping wet when we arrived at the office, and my wet dog stank. In the senator's outer office, I said to a young-sounding voice I heard, "Will you hold my dog's leash while I meet with the senator so Gibney doesn't get the office carpet wet?" Well, it turned out that Gibney's ad hoc caretaker and the senator's legislative aide loved taking care of Gibney, and there's no question the senator respected us for making it to the meeting despite the weather and our rain-soaked condition.

## DOUG:

You and I have spent hundreds of hours working together over the past five years, first on the Lighthouse High-Impact Governing Initiative and later on this book, and we've collaborated on a number of national workshops. During these years, as I've gotten to know you better, I've been impressed by your tremendous passion and energy. What's the source, what really drives you?

## VIRGINIA:

I have to tell you something, Doug, that might sound strange. I feel blessed by my retinitis pigmentosa—by being blind. I didn't ask for it, and I suppose the great majority of people would see it as a curse, or at best a very mixed blessing. I'm not a fatalistic kind of person; you know me well enough to know that I'm not inclined to passively sit back and accept what fate has in store. I'm a doer, an activist to the core! But I've come to believe that God's plan was for me to become blind so I could find a new mission and passion in my work. Do you think that if someone had come to me way back in my Purdue days, before I started losing my sight, and said, "They need a CEO in Miami at a blind agency," I'd have jumped at the job? Assuming I had no vision loss. Assuming that I was 20/20 and playing tennis, and all that. The odds are I wouldn't have been interested.

I would've thought, "Blindness?" I wouldn't have gotten it, I wouldn't have understood what it meant. I wouldn't have related to the Lighthouse clients. I understood students at Purdue. I understood the Purdue mission. But I wouldn't have had a clue about the mission of a social service agency serving the blind. You know, I didn't even pay much attention to, much less understand, the wider world of disabilities. It was really foreign territory to me, and it wasn't until I started to struggle with vision loss that I even thought about people with disabilities. But when I arrived at the Lighthouse in 2001, the door opened to a whole new world, and a tremendous opportunity to make more of a difference than I could ever have made at Purdue, no matter how hard I worked or good I was. I came to the Lighthouse with some really strong skills, especially in finance, and I was blessed to have the opportunity to put them to what I now see as a higher use.

You and I have talked a lot recently about Joseph Campbell's idea of "bliss" [Reader: See Postscript 2]. Well, I've really found my bliss at the Lighthouse. I've found tremendous passion. I can't really say whether I'm called in some way, whether what's happened is part of some kind of divine plan for my life; all I know is I'm blessed to have a passion because a lot of people—maybe most people—go through life without much passion. They just do what they do because they have to do it, because it brings in the paycheck. But I've been given this wonderful opportunity to help blind people get out of the house, so that blind people just don't stay home, so that a senior losing her eyesight knows there is life after blindness, so that a little kid isn't left at this level but learns he can go to that level. The way I see it, there are people in life that are dealt a bad deck of cards for one reason or another, and if they really, really want to do the best that they can, and they try really hard, then they should be able to have the advantages that somebody else has that maybe doesn't even have to work so hard. And I feel like blindness is a pretty bad deck of cards.

You and I have talked about blindness being one of people's greatest fears. But, honestly, at this point in my life if you asked me, "Do you think blindness is one of the worst things that could happen to you?" my answer would be, "If you get the skills that you need there are many worse things. Many worse things."

Let me tell you, my life now is so much fuller than it would've been if I were still at Purdue with my eyesight. Look, how often do you really get to make a tremendous difference in people's lives? Of course, you help your family, you help your kids, but to truly know that you're really making a difference, that's a real privilege, to really make a difference for people who are so grateful, very grateful. Now, I got a lot of satisfaction from my work at Purdue, no question. The joy at Purdue was I had a true customer focus, and the joy was when I knew I really prepared the provost for a meeting with a dean, when I helped get the new school of nursing off the ground, when I was instrumental in getting a clinical pharmacy track going. Those were successes that gave me pleasure and satisfaction, made me proud. But that was a customer focus. That's very different than knowing if you didn't really help this blind person her life would likely be tremendously limited, she'd likely have virtually nothing. I mean, the deans at Purdue, you know, already they were paid nicely, and they were my customers, and you want customer satisfaction. Here it's much more than that. What we're doing at the Lighthouse involves transforming lives. And so you transform somebody from being hopeless when a doctor tells them, "I'm sorry, you're going blind, there's nothing more we can do," to saying to someone, "There's so much more you can do, let us help you learn how." And so that's a real privilege, that's the bliss that Campbell talks about.

Now when I look back on my years at Purdue, I see that whole period as preparation for what I'm doing now. I learned some pretty powerful management skills at Purdue that I've been able to put to good use at the Lighthouse. Take getting grants, for example. I came to the Lighthouse knowing how to strategize to get a grant. So you're thinking about applying to a family foundation for a grant, and you do a little research, and you know that they've made education a top priority, so you know enough not to say to that foundation, "Hey, our seniors in ceramics, we need money for that." Instead, you know they like education, and so you talk to them about, "You know, there's a shortage of vision rehabilitation therapists. There's a growing number of blind people. Miami-Dade needs to have these vision specialists, but Florida State is closing their program. We need to bring interns in from other universities to get them to know about Miami Lighthouse. Would you help fund that?" And so you're focusing on what it is that's going to make them want to fund you. I know how to do that from my Purdue background, so we've been extremely successful in getting grants. Putting my skills to work that way, that's passion, that's real joy, that's Campbell's bliss in concrete terms.

## DOUG:

Virginia, you are one of the more visionary CEOs I've ever worked with, which might be a little ironic since you're blind. Tell me about your vision for the Miami Lighthouse.

## VIRGINIA:

Well, people use the term "vision" in different ways, as you well know, Doug. Lots of people will tell you that a vision should be a very brief statement, maybe two or three sentences, that describe where you want to be in a nutshell. When I use "vision," I mean a really detailed—a multifaceted—picture of what you want your organization to become over the long range, and, in a changing world, that vision is always evolving. So let me paint a not-very-neat picture for you of what I see as the Lighthouse's future. Above all else, my Board and I have a kind of overarching vision of the Lighthouse as a national, maybe even international, center of excellence that's taking a really holistic approach to vision rehabilitation. For one thing, that means not only having mobile eye care units for children who fail vision screening, but also mobile rehabilitation services in Miami-Dade County. I just wrote a proposal to fund a Lighthouse collaboration with the Miami-Dade Public Library: when the Library's bookmobile goes to a senior center our mobile eye care unit goes to the senior center, and when seniors get on the book-mobile they not only get their books, but also a functional eye exam. And if they need to have a vision rehabilitation program, we could have a regular schedule when our mobile unit goes to these different loca-tions, these different libraries. Outreach to seniors, senior centers, and so forth. That's one facet of the Lighthouse vision.

I also see the Lighthouse becoming a national, or perhaps even international, training center for professionals who deal with blind and visually impaired persons, including new professionals such as occupational therapists and ophthalmic nurses. And we've got to ex-tend our educational programming to teachers in the public schools, where there's a tremendous unmet need, and we've got to provide year-round programming for blind and visually impaired kids. If I re-call correctly there are only twelve teachers covering three hundred blind kids in four hundred schools in the Miami-Dade Public Schools, which mainstreams blind students. There's no way they have time to teach these kids Braille, which is the key to learning and a fuller, more productive life for kids blind from birth. Without learning Braille, they'll fall by the wayside, they'll end up being patronized poor little blind kids who grow up to be pathetic older blind people who've been cheated out of a full life. That's wrong; that's really wrong, and the Lighthouse has got to partner with the public schools to prevent that from happening!

My vision for the Lighthouse, as a center of excellence, also includes actively partnering with higher education in lots of possible ways. One is providing academe with research subjects—being a kind of living laboratory—just like my daughter went to the Lighthouse looking for human subjects for her research. We want academics doing research in gerontology, say, or nutrition—whatever—to say, "Oh, let's go to the Lighthouse. Let's do a joint proposal with the Lighthouse." Maybe we have a shared distinguished professorship where the academic appointment is at the university, but the living laboratory is right there at Miami Lighthouse. Technology's another critical piece of the vision puzzle. I want the Miami Lighthouse to be known as a place where new technology is piloted, where we have the latest technology available. Don't forget that technology is by far the most important way to level the playing field for blind and visually impaired people. Imagine me functioning as a really effective CEO without my note taker or JAWS. How would I keep track of discussions in meetings, read and write emails, do spreadsheets? And these are pretty basic things; technological change is galloping ahead, and the Lighthouse has to be right there in the forefront if we aim to be a true center of excellence.

My vision also includes the Lighthouse taking on two really serious unmet needs here in Miami-Dade County. Housing is one of the most pressing; blind people have got the highest rate of homelessness of any disability group. So very often I have to get in touch with a local program for the homeless, and I'm saying something like, "There's this blind person the police called me about who's been evicted, and he's now at the library. They say they brought him to your place, and you said you had a bed, but when you realized the person was blind you said there wasn't a bed." And that happens over and over. Wouldn't it be great if we could buy a building in the area and convert it into housing for the blind? That's certainly part of the evolving vision for the Lighthouse.

The other thing is with our rapidly growing population of visually impaired seniors. One out of four seniors seventy-five years and older will have significant vision loss. They may never be legally blind; however, they'll have vision problems that affect their independent living skills and this is where the growth is, not the legally blind as much. So a senior with macular degeneration will most likely not be legally blind, but might have vision of 20/100 and need our low vision rehabilitation services. This is part of my vision for the Lighthouse of the future—serving more low-vision seniors with rehabilitation services both at the Lighthouse, at senior centers and senior residences. As far as I can tell, retirement communities, assisted living facilities, and nursing homes aren't really prepared to deal with visually impaired people. I think it's likely if I went into one of those retirement homes with a guide dog it would be very difficult to be able to keep that guide dog, probably impossible. How would I get along? So we've got to make sure that institutions in the aging services area are prepared for the rapidly growing number of visually impaired residents that are coming down the pike. Right now, they're definitely not.

I really believe we can turn this vision into reality, not overnight but within the next three or four years. A big part of this is bringing together powerful philanthropists who share the vision and are willing to contribute money to achieving it. I'm talking with my Board about recruiting these philanthropists to serve on what we'll call the

Lighthouse "Vision Council." This will go a long way toward solving the resource piece of the puzzle.

## DOUG:

I know from our work together, Virginia, that you believe in a close working relationship with the Lighthouse Board, so I'm sure you've made a real effort to get the Board involved in visioning. Tell me about that aspect of your CEO job.

## VIRGINIA:

As a CEO, I'm not only guided by the Lighthouse vision, which, as we've discussed, is always evolving, I'm also the point person in making sure that my Board is actively involved with me in shaping the vision and getting it down on paper. Take our center of excellence concept. I spent about a year gathering twenty-five articles about vision, about the shortage of professionals, about the growing numbers of blind Americans, etc. And, of course, I read them through the computer so it's not like I was sitting down reading a sheet of paper, but they're on my computer and they're in print form in a file folder, and so I'm thinking very intently: After reading all of this, where are the nuggets? If we're to become a center of excellence, what initiatives do we need to launch? And so I narrowed the center of excellence concept down to the five key initiatives that appeared most important to me, and then I hired someone to write a white paper on the center of excellence idea, and I gave that person all of the reference materials, and told her, "I want this to be a concept paper that I can give to the Board at a retreat so that the Board can chew on this and decide whether we really do want to become a center of excellence, what it will take to become a center of excellence, and what initiatives have to be launched to make the center a reality."

So this person put together a very impressive concept paper, which was maybe thirty pages long. From that I developed a two-page executive summary, and then that became a Board retreat item. Now the Board's bought into the concept. Getting really high-stakes commitments like that is what being a CEO is all about, in my opinion anyway. Real CEOs don't sit on the sidelines and wait for their board to come up with a vision, and they certainly don't come up with one by themselves; their job is to work closely with their board in coming up with the vision and making sure the board's commitment is firm.

## DOUG:

I have a couple of closing questions, Virginia. First, do you think that losing your sight in middle age over a pretty long period of time has given you a leg-up in your career in any way?

## VIRGINIA:

Oh, there's one obvious advantage of having been sighted for most of my adult life that comes to mind. When you think about when I went to school and began my career, it was much, much more difficult for a blind person to make her way in the world. Expectations were so low—and they're not exactly high now!—and technology was much less advanced. No question: I would've had a much tougher row to hoe, and I probably couldn't have made it as far as I did at Purdue if I'd been blind from birth. In fact, I probably wouldn't have made it to Purdue. And, of course, because I made it so far at Purdue, I was much better prepared—in terms of professional knowledge and experience, especially in finance—for my work at the Lighthouse when the opportunity presented itself.

## DOUG:

Finally, Virginia, we've focused thus far on your overcoming—transcending—your blindness in order to become a highly effective nonprofit CEO. Are there any ways that blindness has actually been an asset to you in your work?

## VIRGINIA:

Well, I think having gone through vision rehabilitation and having experienced it, you can identify very easily with your clients, and they're really your customers. So, Bob will sometimes say, "I've been with my wife so many years, and I still don't understand blindness." Having personally experienced this does make a difference. I also see myself as a role model, helping other blind and visually impaired people, just by being who I am and doing what I do, overcome the stereotype of what a blind person cannot achieve. People who see me can say to themselves, "Oh, there's hope." So if they have a relative or even a senior starting to lose their eyesight to macular degeneration, they don't have to give in to despair or accept some doctor's assessment that "there's nothing you can do." You'd better believe there's something, and I'm living proof!

I think I've become more focused and less distracted by what I call "visual noise" since losing my sight. People sometimes ask me if my hearing has gotten better since becoming blind, and I tell them that's not possible, but I certainly rely more on hearing now, and I certainly hear more than I used to because I'm less distracted. Like when you and I were walking down the sidewalk outside my condo after our first interview session, I didn't know for sure where I was, but I heard the voices of the groundskeepers, and you didn't, probably because you were looking at the scenery. In fact, my hearing's probably not as good as it was a few years ago—oh, the tribulations of getting older!—but I make better use of my ears and so hear more than I used to. And speaking of avoiding distractions, I really do think that not being able to see people's expressions in meetings is another advantage of being blind. I know this might sound a bit far-fetched, but not being able to see negative body language, people rolling their eyes—that kind of thing—means that I'm less easily intimidated in meetings. I'm not the least bit thrown off by skeptical glances or steely gazes, since I don't see them.

I'm sure some of our readers will think I'm stretching a little—maybe a lot—in coming up with benefits of being blind. But why not try to make the best of a difficult situation? I didn't choose to be blind, I wouldn't choose to be blind—of course not! But I am blind; that's it. So, what am I going to do? The way I see it, I can curl up in a ball and focus on what I've lost, or I can charge ahead and try to make a real difference during the time I've been granted. Part of making a difference, to me, is taking whatever advantage I can of losing my sight. That's just who I am, so I don't really have a choice.

# PART THREE

## LESSONS TO SHARE: A DIALOGUE

### REGARDING THIS CLOSING SECTION

This closing section of *The Blind Visionary* consists of a dialogue between the two of us, focusing on four important, very practical lessons that can be gleaned from the Purdue and Lighthouse years that make up Virginia's incredible odyssey:

1. Reach Out Aggressively.

2. Act On Opportunities.

3. Don't Let Fear Win.

4. Keep Things In Perspective.

Although we hope that you have found this account of Virginia's journey interesting and perhaps even inspiring, our preeminent aim in writing this book is to arm you with practical wisdom that you can put to good use in your own life—in charting your own personal and professional journey. The primary measure of our success as authors, in our opinion, is that you are better able to overcome obstacles and capitalize on opportunities in your quest for personal and professional fulfillment, as a result of reading *The Blind Visionary*. This doesn't mean that the lessons we share in this closing section come close to being a step-by-step self-help cookbook of some kind. You, like us, have probably yearned at one time or another for a simple recipe that might extricate you from a tight spot and relieve what feels like unbearable stress. However, you and we know that there are seldom simple answers to complex problems, and concluding with a nice, neat how-to recipe book would not serve you well.

We are also keenly aware that you are you, not Virginia Jacko; you are a unique human being on a journey that is uniquely yours, grappling with your own challenges and opportunities, and guided by your own vision and mission. So not every lesson we discuss in the following dialogue will prove immediately useful to you in building a more rewarding and satisfying personal and professional life, and even the lessons that you can put to work right now will most likely need to be carefully tailored to your unique situation. We also want you to know that we do not see Virginia's odyssey as a learning opportunity exclusively for people who are grappling with awesome challenges with the potential to radically transform their lives, such as the disease that stole Virginia's eyesight. The lessons that we discuss in the dialogue that follows are aimed at the great majority of readers who, while not contending with life-altering crises like Virginia's, nonetheless are confronted over the weeks, months, and years with countless opportunities to take action in response to less dramatic—but nonetheless important—challenges, such as the need to repair a frayed relationship with your spouse or a treasured friend, to acquire new technical skills in order to go for a job that better fits your life's calling, or to overcome your fear of speaking so you are able to share valuable wisdom with the wider world and receive the recognition you deserve.

As we worked on this concluding section, we were reminded of a hilarious 1991 movie *What About Bob?* that, among other things, involves a therapist, played by Richard Dreyfus, who has written a book called *Baby Steps*, laying out a program for incremental personal change, which his obsessive-compulsive patient Bob, played by Bill Murray, takes to heart, driving his therapist crazy in the process. Well, we take no position on the virtues of incremental versus more radical approaches to growing and changing, but we do believe that the lessons we have drawn from Virginia's odyssey apply to all kinds of change, covering the whole spectrum from giant to baby steps, and everything in between.

## LESSON #1: REACH OUT AGGRESSIVELY.

### DOUG:

Virginia, you're one of those really strong, self-reliant people with oodles of self-confidence and discipline who's self-motivated to an extraordinary degree, but you're not even close to being a loner. Au contraire, you're a quintessential people-person who reaches out really aggressively—cultivating allies and building and nurturing networks of relationships. You've also played the ambassadorial role with gusto at the Lighthouse, participating in community events, standing at the podium in forum after forum, and representing the Lighthouse's interests in Tallahassee. So you've taken to heart the prescription that a

CEO should spend no less than one-third and probably more of her time dealing with external relations, but even before you took on the CEO job at the Lighthouse, you were a consummate people-person at Purdue. You reached out to allies like the new president's executive assistant, who showed you around his office for that turning-point briefing session in November 2000, and you cemented really positive working relationships with your key customers at Purdue, most notably the president, provost, vice presidents and deans. I'm sure you'd agree that your tremendous professional success owes a lot to your interpersonal, as well as your diplomatic, skills.

You and I have had two or three really good conversations about a facet of the interpersonal agenda that I call stakeholder-relations management. For our readers' benefit, a stakeholder is a person, group of people, or formal organization that it makes sense to form, nurture, and manage a working relationship with because something important is at stake. It might be support, money, information, or collaboration in the professional sphere, or affection in the personal—whatever. In my consulting business, for example, key stakeholders of mine are clients who hire me and associations that sponsor my speaking and publish my articles and books. Stakeholder-relations management can be kind of like one of those Russian dolls with one enclosed within another, within another, like peeling an onion. For example, the Miami Lighthouse for the Blind was, as my client, an important stakeholder of mine, and within the Lighthouse you, as CEO, and your Board were super-important stakeholders I paid special attention to.

Of course everyone has personal stakeholders who deserve lots of attention in order to keep the relationships healthy—husbands with wives, parents with children, boyfriend with girlfriend, best buddy with best buddy, and on and on. Experience has taught me that two rules make the most difference. For one thing, if a stakeholder relationship is important, which means the stakes involved are significant enough to care much about, then you're well advised to commit a fair amount of time to thinking seriously about, and to managing, the relationship. For another, the best way to keep a relationship healthy is to keep the quid pro quos in balance. What I mean is that I pay attention not only to what I want and need from a particular relationship, but also what I think my stakeholder wants and needs to keep the relationship in balance. To put it rather crudely, "Gimmie, Gimmie, Gimmie" can wear any relationship out. I think our readers would be interested in your take on relationship building generally and on managing relationships with stakeholders, Virginia.

## VIRGINIA:

Let me say first, Doug, that you're absolutely right: I'm no loner, as our readers must know if they've gotten this far in our book. Yeah, I'm an individualist; I'm a pretty strong person with plenty of get-up-and-go and a pretty large dollop of self-discipline, but I'm definitely not what you'd call a loner. One thing I'd like our readers to take away from this book is the importance of reaching out to the people around you in all kinds of ways all the time, building relationships with supporters, stakeholders, collaborators, mentors, whatever. I couldn't have achieved nearly as much at Purdue without really reaching out constantly in all kinds of ways and situations, and, God knows, there's no way I could've gone from vocational rehabilitation student to board member and CEO of the Lighthouse on my own.

OK, you said I should comment on what you call stakeholder management, and I'd be happy to do so. But it would be dishonest of me to pretend that I'm completely comfortable with the term. You've made stakeholder management sound like a pretty formal process that involves calculating quid pro quos to make sure particular relationships stay in balance and don't erode over time. I can see where, as a management consultant, you might advise clients to take this kind of systematic approach to managing relationships with key stakeholders like the agencies that fund them, and, as the Lighthouse CEO, I certainly spend lots of time trying to keep relationships with key stakeholder organizations solid. But what you've got to understand, Doug, is that the great majority of my interactions with people don't have anything to do with formal planning and management. I reach out instinctively because I genuinely like people, and I passionately believe in that golden rule: Treat others as you'd like them to treat you.

Liking people and being caring and considerate probably outweigh everything else in building relationships with the people around you. I don't consciously think of the drivers who take me to work in the morning as stakeholders I'm managing; they're just people I like and whose help I really appreciate, and they know it. I hope I'd be polite and friendly whether I needed their help or not, but the fact is, I can pick up the phone anytime and get one of the drivers to take me someplace, and I'm sure it's because I treat them with consideration. But there are a couple of other factors that I think have helped me tremendously in reaching out. For one thing, I'm who I am—what you see is what you get—whatever the situation I'm in. I think people want to know that you're not putting on one mask or another, depending on who you're with at a particular time. That's what being authentic means, and one thing I've learned over the years is that most people really do want to know that they're dealing with the one real you, not some mask you've put on for the occasion. Another thing is, I feel truly passionate about the Lighthouse mission, and I think my passion comes through loud and clear to people, and is kind of like a magnet that attracts them to me. Well, you can't calculate being caring, authentic, and passionate, but they're in my experience the top three relationship builders.

You know, Doug, thinking about two women who each gave approximately a million dollars to the Lighthouse, I didn't carefully cultivate them as stakeholders—as potential donors—over a period of time. Their generous donations, which have made a tremendous difference, didn't have anything to do with some kind of methodical stakeholder-management process, to use your lingo. What happened is that each of them was brought to the Lighthouse by a volunteer at different times, and we connected immediately. I think they sensed that I wasn't just being friendly to take advantage of an opportunity, I wasn't trying to manipulate them, and I know from what they've told me that my passion for the Lighthouse mission had a powerful impact. We've become good friends because we share a passionate belief in transforming the lives of people who've come to the Lighthouse for help.

Poor Doug, you probably feel like I've kind of bashed your stakeholder management idea, but that wasn't the idea. I just wanted to make clear that there are some really important basics in dealing with the people around you that don't involve calculating quid pro quos and formally managing relationships. They make up a fundamental foundation, whatever kind of relationship you're thinking about. But I really do see the usefulness of consciously managing many professional relationships involving what you might call stakeholders. Of course, our clients—our students—at the Lighthouse are important stakeholders, that kind of goes without saying. We owe them high-quality programming in exchange for their time and willingness to try hard. And there's my Board, which is definitely a top-priority stakeholder I pay a lot of attention to. One reason we got into the governance project that you and I worked on is that I felt I owed my Board a really top-notch governing experience. They're not paid in money for all the time and attention they're giving, so I make sure they're paid in a different currency: really important work to do on the Board and well-designed committees to help them do it. That's the least I can do, when you think of how important the Board is, not only to the Lighthouse generally, but to me as CEO.

And the world outside the Lighthouse is filled with very important stakeholders, way too many for me to manage on my own, but I do pay pretty close attention to a lot of them, including important funders like the state of Florida and here locally the Health Foundation of South Florida and the Children's Trust. At the very least, I make sure that the Lighthouse religiously follows grant requirements, including getting our funders the reports they want—complete and on time. But more than that, I go out of my way to stay in touch with the chief honchos at these organizations, and many others, because one-on-one relationships matter. Organizations are people, right? Not some kind of abstract thing. You know, I think of my CEO job at the Lighthouse as Relationship-Builder-in-Chief, along with all the other things I've got to keep me busy. If I had twenty more hours a week to give, maybe fifteen or more of those hours would go to keeping my key stakeholders happy.

I do, of course, take the initiative to consciously cultivate a relationship when I've identified a person as a critical stakeholder whose input and support we need. For example, when the Lighthouse merged the Heiken Children's Vision Program into our operation, I launched an advisory board composed of the stakeholders who would be most important for the merger to become a true synergy, such as foundation CEOs, community optometrists, the former chairs of the Heiken Board, and the like. There was one doctor, an internationally known optometrist, who wasn't any longer active in the Heiken leadership group, but I was told it was important for me to get him involved in the new advisory board that we'd established. The first two times I phoned his office, I wasn't able to get through to him, but we connected on the third call, and I told him about my vision for the Miami Lighthouse Heiken Children's Vision Program and the new advisory board we'd established, and I said we really needed him on the board. When he responded that he was too busy, I said that I'd like to mail him the minutes of each advisory board meeting, and should he have any questions or thoughts as to how we could continue to provide good service to low-income kids who fail their school vision screening, he was always welcome to join us at a board meeting. So I did that, and about three advisory board meetings later he showed up and ever since has been crucial to our synergistic relationship with optometrists. In fact, this year he has donated more than $70,000 of pro bono service by providing us special software and by making all the prescription glasses—more than five thousand this year—at almost no cost to us. That's stakeholder management, right Doug?

Before turning it back to you, Doug, I'd like to say a word about another side of this stakeholder management thing: investing in future relationships even though you're not certain what they'll evolve into, or what the concrete payoff will be. What you're betting on is that making friends and allies is likely to result in some kind of bottom-line benefit down the pike, even if it means no more than just being able to pick up the phone and picking a colleague's brain on an issue. I can think of a recent example: the Alliance for Aging here in Miami. When the Alliance was putting together a transportation proposal, they were looking for a partner and their CEO got in touch with me. At first, I said to myself, "No way; we've got a thousand other things on our plate we've got to deal with in the near future, so how can we take on something else, especially something that's kind of outside our main focus?" But on second thought, I figured that down the road a bit it might be very important to have the Alliance as an ally, and so I signed on as a partner in getting the proposal put together. And when it turned out that we needed to participate in a trip to Washington to help sell the proposal, I couldn't go, but I sent one of my senior executives in my place. As it turns out, alliance building in this case has paid off in terms of a valuable new relationship, even though we don't know where it will take us in the future. My motto? Reach out, reach out, reach out, and then reach out some more! You can't have too many happy stakeholders and loyal friends and allies. You might not know when you'll need to work together on something, it could come up in an instant, with no warning, so turning stakeholders into allies can't wait until you need them; that can be way too late.

## DOUG:

We haven't spent any time talking about the personal side of stakeholder relations, Virginia. My guess is that a lot of people don't pay close enough attention to personal stakeholder relationships, maybe because they tend to take them for granted. I had an experience several years ago that brought this point home to me. My son, William, who, if I recall correctly, was then eleven, and I drove from Cleveland, Ohio, to the Detroit, Michigan, area, where we dropped my daughter, Jennifer, off at her lacrosse camp and then checked into a hotel near Greenfield Village, where we planned to spend the next day. The next morning at breakfast, I was enthusiastically laying out our itinerary, pointing to different spots on the map I'd spread out on the table, when I noticed that William had fallen really quiet and was looking pretty morose. So when our breakfast came, I shut up and asked myself what was going on. Without really thinking about what I was doing, I went through a quick stakeholder quid-pro-quo analysis: My only real need, I thought to myself, was for William to have a good time and be a happy tour companion. What he needed was to have a good time, but I knew him well enough to realize that that wasn't likely to happen if he didn't have a real voice in mapping out our day together. So I said, "William, I've shared some ideas, but why don't you take it from here and put together the plan for the day, and I mean the whole day—what we see when, where we eat, the whole shebang." You should've seen his eyes light up. We had a wonderful time, and I learned a valuable lesson about personal stakeholder relations!

Now, let's turn to a different dimension of reaching out: looking for mentors and role models. Thinking about your Purdue and Lighthouse experiences, Virginia, it's clear to me that you've been a lifelong learner par excellence. You've done a great job of reaching out to people you think you can learn from, like the nonprofit CEO early in your CEO tenure at the Lighthouse who advised you to stay close to home until you'd gotten things really humming along, and only then start traveling to conferences and meetings around the country. You and I met when you reached out for help in developing the Lighthouse Board into a more effective governing body and in building a really solid Board-CEO working relationship.

## VIRGINIA:

There's absolutely no question that one of the big reasons why I've been successful as CEO of the Lighthouse is that I've been willing to call on outside help when I've thought I needed it. Even if I knew every last thing I needed to know to be a successful CEO—and you'd better believe I don't!—I wouldn't have the time to accomplish all of the things that need to be done. Take, for instance, the need to help Lighthouse staff understand the importance of thinking more like entrepreneurs than traditional social workers—thinking about innovative ways to tap new resource streams and not just rely on the same old government programs. We've made lots of progress in becoming what people these days call "social entrepreneurs," but I couldn't have begun to change the traditional social work mentality by myself. I hired a consultant, in this case the former CEO of a major blind services agency who had a PhD in nursing. She's a sharp, sharp woman who understands that the Lighthouse has to become a social enterprise, not just an old-time agency, if we hope to grow in the future, and she's met with my key managers to help them understand the need to change how we think about our work at the Lighthouse.

Governance is another area where I couldn't have accomplished our really essential modernization of the Lighthouse Board's committee structure without the help of a consultant with years of hands-on experience in working with nonprofit boards and, equally important, the credibility of an outside expert the Board would take seriously. To bring a consultant on board involved some risk, because some Board members might have said, "Who the heck do you think you are telling us that we need help? We think we're just fine. The problem is yours." But any self-respecting CEO has to be willing to take the risk and be able to say, "This is the right thing to do, and I'm willing to go out on the limb to get it done." I've already said that I couldn't have succeeded as CEO without serious development of my Board as a governing body. Even thinking about having to run around working with the twelve different Board committees I inherited gives me the chills. So bringing in a consultant was a no-brainer, but it still took a bit of courage on my part, if I do say so.

And it's not just a matter of hiring experts. Finding mentors and really paying attention to what they have to teach is a low-cost/high-yield strategy that I recommend to all our readers, no matter what they're engaged in. Of course, using mentors requires choosing the right teachers and taking the time to learn, but it still doesn't cost you any money. I've been on the lookout for mentors since my earliest days at Purdue, and it's really paid off. You know, Doug, there's only so much you can learn from books, or in classrooms. Some of the most valuable knowledge I've acquired over the years has come from watching and listening. In terms of my job as CEO, when I have to handle a situation, I often think about the former president of Purdue, Steven Beering, who's now chair of the National Science Board of the National Science Foundation. I've said to myself more than once, "How would Steven Beering handle this?" And I think of times like when he went up to Indianapolis with a Purdue delegation to present something they wanted the legislature to act on, and they didn't get what they wanted. After they got back to Purdue, I dropped by the office of the vice president for state relations and his team and said, "Hey, how did everything go yesterday?" And they responded with something like, "Oh, it didn't go very well." And then I went to see the president and asked how things had gone the day before. He responded with something like, "You know, we're going to get them to go along next year. We planted the seed, and we're going to get it next year." Things like this happened more than once. Steven Beering taught me a wonderful lesson about not only thinking positively, but about persevering, not giving up just because things don't go your way in a particular instance.

My Lighthouse Board members aren't just stakeholders that I've got to manage a relationship with; they're also my trusted colleagues and teachers. Sure, they're my boss, but I think of them as a huge asset—a tremendous collection of knowledge and expertise that they can share with me on an as-needed basis. Take my current Board chair, Owen Freed. He was a very active leader in Rotary in

Miami, had been a district governor, and we got to know each other when the Lighthouse honored the Miami Rotary Club at its 75th anniversary gala in 2006. Since he's become chair of the Lighthouse Board, he's become a trusted advisor and teacher, and it's great that his office is nearby. He likes to pick up the phone and ask me how things are going, and there've been a few times I've had to say, "Owen, I think we've got an issue here that I'd like to bounce off you." By the way, I don't for an instant worry about maybe seeming weak because I'm asking for help; I can't worry about trivial ego things like that. I'd much rather have Owen's or some other Board member's best thinking on an issue, than trying to make them think I'm always in command and never need help.

And the current chair of our Board's external relations committee, Ray Casas, is a highly successful public relations and marketing CEO who's full of great ideas—a real pro. So I've felt free to tap into his experience and wisdom several times; I've made him an important mentor.

For example, when he interviewed a candidate for our development director position, at my invitation, he was able to give me feedback that made a real difference; he could see past the formal credentials and interpersonal skills and give me insights based on years of experience that I didn't bring to the table. I can't tell how valuable that was in making such an important personnel decision. I could give you other examples of Board members whose experience and expertise I've tapped into since I've been CEO, and I'll be on the lookout for new Board mentors as long as I'm there.

I'm also pretty lucky that I've had important mentors close to home, and my husband, Bob, is at the top of the list. Time and again, I've relied on him for important advice at critical times, and he's always come through. Let me give you an example from my Purdue days. I was working on my master's then, and I had to take calculus, which was a pretty big deal since I'd been away from math for quite some time. At the time, Bob was an assistant professor working his way up the academic ladder, and you'd better believe he didn't have a minute to spare. Anyway, I ran into immediate trouble because I couldn't understand the teacher in my calculus class, and I was feeling kind of overwhelmed. Not only did Bob help me choose a new section, where I'd have a teacher I could follow more easily, he also pitched in himself. After I'd changed my section, Bob said to me, "Look. It's been a while since you've had math. I'll make a deal with you. Don't drop calculus. Every lunch hour come to my office, and we'll work on your calculus together." I'm happy to report that I did well in the course, with Bob's help. He's definitely one of my prize mentors!

I've got to tell you something about my parents, who were great mentors who taught me some really valuable things by example. My mother, who's ninety-four now, was studying nursing in Chicago when she and my dad got married. She wanted to stay in Chicago to finish her degree, and then she was asked to stay on and teach, so my parents decided to live in Evanston, north of the city. Back then there was a train that ran from Chicago to Racine, so my dad would take the train to Racine to go to work, and my mom would take the train to downtown Chicago. And my mother recently told me that, you know, being a good Catholic within ten months or so of getting married, she was pregnant. She said that her mother took care of my older sister until I came along a year later, and she decided she needed to be back in Racine raising her growing family. That was pretty daring for those times. Women just didn't do that.

And then she had five children, all very accomplished kids—an architect, an economics professor, a periodontist, etc.—but my mother decided to go back to school and her teaching career, so she got a master's degree during that time period, and then went back to work. She was the director of nurses at a local nursing school, and she headed up the health occupations division for the state technical college system for the southern half of Wisconsin. Model and mentor, that's my mother. She was a great model for balancing work and family. I think she struggled a little bit because her role was different than women of that generation, and to this day probably struggles with that because she was such a forerunner. So, it began with my mother. I told you the story about her urging me to "forget this half-time stuff, go full time," when I was just getting started up the ladder at Purdue.

Now, my dad was then vice president of a manufacturing company, and the summer I was fourteen and a high school student, he came home and said, "Virginia, the sales manager's secretary just quit, and I told FM [the president of the company] that it would be a great summer job for you, so you're going to be working for him as his secretary this summer." Dad gave me some pretty sound advice before my first day on the job: "Look, here's a couple of rules. You don't take a coffee break and you don't sit around and talk about everybody else, or spread gossip, or talk about your personal life. When you're at work, it's all business." So, that was a good early lesson. And I'll never forget the time that the firm's president walked into the sales manager's office looking for a particular document. Well, I was responsible for filing things, and I couldn't find it. So the president picked up my waste basket, dumped it on my desk, and said, "Look, maybe you can find it in here." And he probably prefaced the whole thing, I don't remember for sure, by saying "Girl." Well, that certainly wouldn't be considered politically correct these days, but it was still a valuable lesson and it kind of toughened me up for things to come years hence.

## DOUG:

It's interesting how much we have in common, Virginia; that's probably one of the main reasons it's been so easy for us to work together in writing this book. We really do share a lot. My mother, you know, had six kids and went back to college in her forties when five of us kids were still at home. She started with a correspondence course from, if I recall correctly, Indiana University—there weren't community colleges in those days—and I have vivid memories of her studying and writing papers at the dining room table in the wee hours, sometimes as late as 3 a.m. She eventually attended a small private college some thirty miles away, and became a very fine special English teacher who ran labs for kids who were having trouble learning English. OK, time to get back to our main agenda.

In Part Two, you told about spending quite a bit of time serving as an ambassador for the Miami Lighthouse in events around the Greater Miami community, first as a volunteer and later as the Lighthouse CEO, including your fascinating stories about participating in the Humane Society fashion show and the time you came close to falling down the escalator at a gala you were attending. And I know that you're a very in-demand speaker, who's spoken all over the community on behalf of the Lighthouse, in all kinds of forums. As a person who struggled with tremendous performance anxiety two decades ago when I began my consulting and public speaking career, I really respect anyone who is willing to stand at the podium and expose herself to listeners' judgments. But a speaker who's blind certainly faces some special challenges, like how to show PowerPoint slides, for example. Talk a bit about this part of your external role.

## VIRGINIA:

You know that I'm pretty comfortable on the platform. I've probably mentioned that I was a champion debater in high school who went to college on a debate scholarship, so it's been years since I had to deal with any fears about public speaking. Thinking back all those years, it's interesting that I've become so comfortable at the podium since I was quite a shy little girl, one of those smart little kids who was afraid to raise my hand in elementary school, but I was pretty well over that by the fifth or sixth grade. Anyway, standing up and talking to a crowd seems pretty natural, in fact, I love it. One thing our readers might be interested in hearing about is how I handle PowerPoint slide presentations as a totally blind CEO. You might think the answer's simple: I read the slide text in Braille while I'm presenting the slides, but that doesn't work for me. Keep in mind that the really good Braille users that read as quickly as a sighted person typically are born blind, and to them Braille is like a native language. Like if Spanish is your first language, you're going to be able to read Spanish quicker than anyone that has studied Spanish as a second language, that is, unless they've worked really, really hard at mastering Spanish. And so when people say to me, "Can you read Braille?" I say, "You know, I read it, but like a kindergartner."

If I'm giving a presentation using PowerPoint there's no way I'd have time to read Braille text by touching those various combinations of dots—or bumps—with the tip of my finger. Think about it: I'd be using my finger in a space about the size of a sixteen-point font, and I'd be saying, oh, in cell number one there's a dot. That's an a. Oh, but wait a minute. Right before that in cell number three there's a dot that means it's a capital A. So your mind has to go through a lot of different thoughts in order to figure out what the tip of your finger's feeling. You'd have to have oodles of practice for it to become second nature.

In my student days at the Lighthouse, I didn't have time to become a really capable Braille user; shame on me, but I just haven't had the time. So how do I, as a blind person, use PowerPoint? Well, I do a lot of memorizing, which might seem really difficult, but practice does make you a lot better at it. Here's the process: first I type out my presentation, then I make an outline of the presentation, and using that outline, I come up with key words, after which I come up with acronyms for the key words, which I memorize. Take, for example, my progress report to the Lighthouse Board on CEO targets. I can't read what I'm going to tell the Board Operations Committee my various achievements were under each one of my major target areas for that quarter. But I have in my mind the first letter of the acronym for each of the target areas, and under each of those targets I have an acronym based upon key words for the four or five items that I want to tell them about.

So for the key target areas external relations, finance, and human relations, I have the acronym "EFH," which I change to the easier-to-recall "HEF," which I memorize, giving me the main target areas I'm reporting on. The process is the same for the sub-categories I'm talking about under each target area. So I'm creating and memorizing a series of acronyms, which help me recall content, which I work really hard to know inside out. I know that sounds horribly complicated, but I'm used to it since I'm getting constant practice, and it's working if audience comments I hear mean anything, and that's what matters.

## LESSON #2: ACT ON OPPORTUNITIES.

### DOUG:

I know that you relate as strongly as I do, Virginia, to Viktor Frankl's conception of fundamental "meaning" as a pairing of purpose or calling with action. And the two of us are in complete agreement with Frankl that we can find meaning from acting on an opportunity even when the circumstances are so constraining that just the tiniest action is possible. Intent isn't enough, right? It's action that fuels meaning. No one's ever said this better than Allen Wheelis in *How People Change* [Reader: See Postscript 2]. You and I loved a passage from *How People Change*, which I'd like to read if you don't mind. Here it is: "A farmer must know the fence which bounds his land but need not spend his life standing there, beating his fists on the rails; better he till his soil, think of what to grow, and where to plant the fruit trees. However small the area of freedom, attention and devotion may expand it to occupy the whole of life." Amen! Call me squishy, but I can't read this without feeling teary-eyed, it's so moving, so optimistic.

No one would ever accuse you of being a passive bystander, Virginia; you've led an extraordinarily action-packed life. Not just busy, but opportunistic in the best sense of that word. Your story, at Purdue and later at the Lighthouse, is about pouncing on opportunities, not sitting back and pondering pros and cons endlessly. "Paralysis by analysis" is a malady you've never suffered, as far as I can tell. Candidly, I've wondered if you might've been a bit precipitous now and then, but your track record speaks for itself: moving from a part-time to full-time position at Purdue; taking medical leave and heading to the Miami Lighthouse; resigning from Purdue to go through guide dog training in New York City; joining the Lighthouse Board; becoming interim and then permanent CEO; and on and on. This is life in the fast lane!

Why don't you begin by talking about your approach to making decisions, especially the ones that appear to be snap decisions that might be really risky?

## VIRGINIA:

You've probably heard the saying, "There are those who are presented with an opportunity, and they don't see it. And then there are those who see the opportunity, but they're afraid to act on it." I like to think that over the years I've compiled a pretty good track record of not only spotting opportunities for action, but also acting. And I'm not one to sit around agonizing over decisions; as you've pointed out, Doug, you're not apt to catch me laboriously going through every last pro and con. That's just not my style. But I want you to know that I don't— I really don't—make snap judgments, I'm not inclined to take stupid risks. And that's true of some of the more dramatic decisions we've talked about that might seem really impulsive, like when I called Bob about getting the sabbatical so we could head to Miami and I could enroll in the Lighthouse, or when I called the president at Purdue and told him I wouldn't be coming back, that I'd be heading for New York for guide dog training. You know, I never even discussed that with Bob. I made the phone call, and he came home, and I told him. But you'd be wrong if you thought I'd made snap judgments in either instance. I actually made pretty well-informed decisions that just seemed to come out of the blue. In reality, I had the pros and cons in mind when I decided what to do, I just didn't need to agonize over them.

The way my mind works is I'm always gathering information. I'm not dwelling on it, but it's kind of like I have a little computer folder in my brain, and I'm constantly putting things in that folder, but I'm not going to that folder until I need to. There's a wealth of information in that folder that I've accumulated, so that when I need to make a decision, it comes into play. That's what was happening as I was slowly losing my vision at Purdue; I started to store information in my internal computer folder about resources for people who are blind and visually impaired. So when the time is right, I've got lots of information stored away, and I'm able to draw on it to make a quick decision. It's not like I'm running off half-cocked. I don't think I've ever run off half-cocked. At Purdue, I knew as my sight got worse and worse that I was going to be vulnerable, that I'd probably not be able to continue in my job someday, so I was storing up the information I'd need when I had to make a decision.

Another thing is, I'm always looking for ways to turn challenges into opportunities for action. Okay, I'll give you one example. The

Lighthouse had a grant from a funder that'd been really faithful to us, and I was trying to position the Lighthouse to get what's called a "signature grant" from this funder. This is a large grant that's made only every few years, and it naturally requires that you follow the rules to the letter, including getting in your grant renewal proposal on time. Only those who play by the rules are eligible, right? Well, I figured we'd done everything necessary to position ourselves to get the grant; I was even invited to attend the funder's board meeting as an outside observer, which seemed to be a great sign. So I go to the board meeting, which includes dinner, and during dinner I'm sitting next to the CEO's secretary who says to me: "Virginia, today was the deadline for the proposal renewal, and we never got a proposal from the Lighthouse." You can imagine how shocked I was. For the rest of the meeting I had to be very personable, but on the inside, I'm dying.

The next morning when I got to the office, I was pretty steamed. I called together my senior managers, and I didn't beat around the bush, believe me. I said something like, "OK guys, we've got a chief financial officer, a head of grants and grant compliance, and we've got a director of programs on our team. We've also got a calendar of grant deadlines. Last night I found out that our renewal proposal was due yesterday, and we missed the boat. Now, we're not going to spend time right now talking about how it happened." I told them I'd be seeing the CEO of the funding agency at one o'clock that afternoon and that I intended to arrive at that meeting with both the proposal and my hat in my hand. I laid out the marching orders: "We take last year's proposal. We look at what our numbers were. We cut and paste, and so-and-so works on all the attachments, our nonprofit statement, last year's audited financials, and we all pitch in because at noon I'm leaving this office, and I'm going to have that proposal in hand." And when one of my staff popped in a few minutes to tell me that they weren't really certain about the number of children who'd been served, I said, "You know what? It doesn't matter if we have to go back later and say we need to adjust the numbers; just give it your best shot, and that's the number of kids we'll say we're going to serve because we just don't have time to pin it down for a certainty. We're going to just use our best estimate."

I'll bet you a lot of CEOs would've just chewed their people out and left it at that, but at one o'clock on the button, I was in the CEOs office. After telling her how much I appreciated being at their board meeting the night before, and chitchatting for a couple of minutes, I said, "I'm here because we've had a major goof—a really major goof, and I take full responsibility for it. You set me up beautifully with your board, but we didn't get our renewal proposal in on time, shame on us." And I said, "I'm very sorry, and there's no point in my explaining why it happened; it just did. But you got our last report on our progress and you know that we've doubled the number of children we serve." She said, "Absolutely, your progress report was great." And I said, "I just ask that you consider including our proposal in the packet you'll be presenting to your board. That's all I can ask; I know you can't guarantee anything." And she said, "I'll give it my best shot." And we got the funding; it was a happy ending, because we took action—fast.

One of my staff later told me, "Virginia, you'll never take no from anyone, will you?" I responded that I didn't think that's what it was about. "I think it's about turning a challenge into an opportunity, and opportunities can change the course of events."

## DOUG:

One of the things that's struck me as we've worked together over the past four years or so is that you're not just decisive and action-focused, you're also one of those rare leaders who's a true innovator. You see possibilities for action that many people might not see, and you turn those possibilities into concrete innovations. Talk about your role as what you might call the "chief innovation officer" of the Lighthouse.

## VIRGINIA:

I think being a creative decision maker has been tremendously important to my success at the Lighthouse. I can't tell you how much joy it gives me to expand the good we do at the Lighthouse by doing what I call changing the problem, another skill that I honed during my Purdue years. I'm pretty certain that we're going to be awarded a large grant from a major foundation for our music program at the Lighthouse. That will be so great. The idea's to teach blind students what they need to know to get mainstream employment as music producers. And if we get the grant, I've already got the University of Miami Frost School of Music on board. I have a faculty member and PhD student from Frost here this summer. We got them by changing the problem; here's what happened. We'd received a foundation grant, and I could get another $25,000 from the foundation if I used it for graduate students from the Frost School of Music. But we needed to spend the entire amount by the project's end. So I spoke to the people at the foundation, and they said, "Oh, but the university said the graduate students wouldn't start until the last month of the grant." The foundation people told me, "Tell the Frost School to bill you, and you write the full check now out of this money because it won't roll over."

So I told the dean at the Frost School about it, and when they went to their business office, the people there said, "No, we can't do that." And so I called the business office, kind of talked to them, and I realized that these are really firm guys. And the dean says, "I'm so sorry, but this isn't going to work." And the foundation says, "We're so sorry it's not going to work." And I thought about it, and I called the dean back, and I said, "Hey, are all of your faculty paid twelve months?" And he said, "Oh, no. Ten months." I said, "Do you have any PhD students? Are they paid during the summer?" He said there weren't. And I said, "Well, let's forget the scholarships and the research assistantships, since they'll require going beyond the grant expiration, and I need to spend that money this summer." The upshot was that the Lighthouse directly hired a Frost faculty member and graduate student for the summer, which meant we could use the full grant amount by the expiration date. And so I changed my problem. Sometimes people say, "Virginia won't accept no." But it's not that I won't accept no. You need to be able to change your problem so that you can make it work. To me, that's creative decision making; that's what gets serious innovation accomplished, even though it's about as far from traditional strategic planning as possible.

## DOUG:

Before we move on to the next lesson, Virginia, would you comment on something I've heard you say a couple of times during our interview sessions: that being blind has been an asset insofar as your creativity is concerned. The first time I heard you say that, I said to myself, "Sure she says that; she's a true half-glass-full person if there ever was one. But that can't literally be true; Virginia, bless her heart, is a virtuoso at turning problems into opportunities, that's how she's gotten so far." So tell me, my dear coauthor, do you really mean what you said?

## VIRGINIA:

Absolutely, Doug. I really do believe that I've become more creative in my work since becoming blind for the simple reason that I'm not bothered by as many distractions. My gut feel is it's because I'm not distracted by what I call visual noise. You know, sight is such a powerful sense that it can bombard you with visual sensations, which doesn't happen to me, of course. I read a tremendous amount, by the way, using things like books and journals on tape, but because I'm not distracted by a lot of other visual input, I spend more time actually thinking and solving creative problems than I did when I could see. You and I have talked about how people these days seem to spend so much time texting each other that they're probably writing and reading more and faster, and thinking less. I think that's almost certainly true. You know, I'm really involved in all of the major public relations pieces we generate at the Lighthouse, whether we're talking about our annual report, whether we're talking about a direct marketing appeal, a letter to an important donor, or our newsletter. Lots of the basic ideas come from me because we haven't hired a fancy, high-priced marketing/public relations person.

Take our annual report this year; the cover features a piece of ceramic that our children made with a visiting artist in summer camp, and it's now hanging on the wall at the Lighthouse. Every kid made a little piece of a ceramic, and it was all put together in a wonderful huge ceramic collage. When I "saw" it the first time, I mean I touched it, of course, it was wow, this makes such a statement about each one of these forty children. So the next time our photographer was at the Lighthouse for an event, I said, "Could you take different photos of this, high contrast, because I've decided this is going to be the next cover of our annual report." I really think in my sighted life, there were often many things that I could see and read so quickly that I'd easily get distracted. It's too much information. And so I've been told that the cover of our annual report is incredible. Now, someone might find what I've just told you hard to believe; they'd doubt that a blind person could've seen the cover. But I did see it. I saw it with my hands by touching these different pieces. And when it comes to writing the annual report I'm thinking about the most important things that we did, what focus will really grab our donors, and then I'm outlining what I'd like it to look like, before I turn the thing over to a professional writer to put it all together. But almost all of what I'm going to call our creative content comes from something that is actually born in my mind through something that gave me a visual picture in my mind. But, of course, I never saw it with my eyes, but I either saw it through my hearing or saw it through my touch.

## Lesson #3: Don't Let Fear Win.

### Doug:

As you've been talking about turning challenges into practical, down-to-earth opportunities for innovation, Virginia, I've wondered where courage fits into this picture. Being courageous obviously has something to do with taking actions that involve newness and possibly major risks, certainly the risk of failing. It's clear to me that taking important actions isn't just the result of some kind of logical decision-making process. If all we had to do is logically think things through, methodically weighing pros and cons, we'd get off pretty easily, but I know you'll agree that it's not just the head, as they say; the heart's a big factor, too. By "heart," I'm talking about the emotional side of things. In my work as a consultant over the years, I've come to think of courage as a kind of mental fuel that helps us get past fears of one kind or another, whether a person's worried about getting hurt physically, or afraid of some kind of emotional damage, like embarrassment or, much worse, humiliation. I've concluded from my experience that being creative and doing significantly new things can call for lots of courage. And don't you agree that the higher the stakes involved in taking some kind of action, the more we're likely to need to call on courage to take us past whatever fears might slow us down, or even bring us to a screeching halt?

I've got to say, my friend, that you're easily one of the gutsiest people I've ever known; you're blessed with a really extraordinary dollop of courage. I'm sure most of our readers, learning about your Purdue and Lighthouse experiences, would say that it took tremendous courage for you to keep going at Purdue for so long while your eyesight was failing. Correct me if I'm wrong, but it must have seemed a lot riskier to ask for a medical leave and head into a totally different environment, the Lighthouse, where you actually started all over again. One month you're a senior, really successful financial executive working in an environment you know inside out, then—whammo!—only a few weeks later, you're a lowly student who not only isn't sure what you'll be studying, but also isn't really certain how you'll be putting this new knowledge to use down the road a few months. You think it'll be back at Purdue, but you're not certain, and you've suggested that by that time you realized going back to West Lafayette might not work out.

Doing those things, that's real courage, to my mind. As you pointed out in one of our interview sessions, you didn't have to put yourself in a totally new situation so that you could earn a living. You could've retired pretty comfortably in West Lafayette without serious money worries, but, instead, you took on one challenge after another after you made that dramatic decision to take medical leave and head to Miami. You really did take risks. You could've failed, you had plenty of opportunities to fall on your face—I mean figuratively, but I guess you could've literally, too—and to be really embarrassed, but you managed to conquer whatever fears you might've had in order to move on, take action. I'm really curious to know where all that courage came from, where it comes from.

### VIRGINIA:

First of all, you've got to believe in yourself. If you really do believe in yourself, that you're able to accomplish whatever you set out to do, whatever fears you're facing are going to seem less threatening. That's certainly my experience. But I don't want you to think I've always been this brave kind of person who just charges ahead and does what I've set out to do. I don't claim to be this courageous superwoman. I've been afraid, and there've been times I haven't gotten past my fears or doubts, when I haven't believed in myself enough. Remember when I was a student at the Lighthouse and heard the CEO was leaving, and I talked with a counselor about maybe applying for the job, and she talked me out of it? I definitely didn't believe in myself enough then. Let me give you another example, back in West Lafayette before I even got my part-time job at Purdue.

You know that I've got a really solid financial background, and did back then—understanding investments and personal finance, always being on top of all the different laws that relate to taxes. It was kind of my vocation or hobby, reading *Money* magazine and getting to know all this kind of stuff about wills, and mortgages, and whatever, things that the average person is interested in, trying to be financially smart. So I came up with this idea, that I'd love to have a radio show dealing with personal finances. This was something I could do while still taking care of the kids, and I knew that I'd be good at it, but I didn't listen to that voice inside telling me to go for it. And that is something I say to myself to this day when I think about it, "You really could have done that, Virginia, you're good with words, you're a debater, and you love numbers, but you didn't have enough faith in yourself. You just didn't believe." I was afraid, I guess, because I didn't know enough about it. How do you get on a radio show? How do you write for *Money*? So I hadn't matured enough to have the self-confidence to say, "Make a few phone calls, create some relationships, find out what it's all about and then just do it." Fear won then, for certain.

You and I have talked about the importance of being a positive thinker, you know, like Norman Vincent Peale's "power of positive thinking" and Wayne Dyer's "power of intention." Maybe it's kind of too obvious to mention, but I really do think that being a positive thinker has helped me get over fears. It's really close to the idea of believing in myself. I don't think I'm being—what do you call it?—a Pollyanna, when I try to see the glass half full. To me, it's simple: You waste precious time and energy on negative thoughts. You've only got so much energy and you've only got so much time. And so you can choose how you spend your time. You can choose how you spend your thoughts. And so spending much time on something negative is not really productive. And I really think it comes more from that attitude than that I'm such a bubbly, Everything's Okay! type. Because I don't think that really is me; I've always been a pretty hard-headed realist. But that doesn't mean I'm negative. I just think that when you see a bump in the road you assume you can deal with it, you don't expect it to defeat you. So you tackle the bump realistically, you get over the bump, and you go on. Because that's your life. That's life. That's what it is.

## DOUG:

Do you remember, Virginia, when we first starting batting around the concept of mission as an important part of your story? I think it popped up during our first interview session back in December 2008, when we were talking about what you really loved about your work at Purdue and why you went to such lengths to keep working while your sight kept getting worse. And we've talked about your mission being one of the most important reasons why finally giving up the role that you'd worked so hard to create at Hovde Hall was such an excruciating decision. We weren't using the term in the conventional planning sense (you know, like a pithy paragraph describing what we're all about as an organization), but in a more personal way that we've never in all our interview sessions tried to pin down very precisely. You correct me if I don't get this completely right, but as I see it, we've been talking about mission as a sense of fundamental purpose—a kind of calling—that gives greater meaning to the work we're engaged in, right? It's what guides and makes sense of the choices we make day after day, and it's what keeps us energized and able to keep moving even when things aren't going well, like a light at the end of a tunnel that helps us persevere through the darkness.

You're probably one of the most ambitious people I've come across over the years, and God knows, you've been successful, but I'm 99 percent sure you'd second the notion that just shooting high and working hard don't cut it over the long haul. Without a pretty good sense of why, at a really fundamental level, you're engaged in whatever job you're doing—what contribution you're aiming to make—you're just as likely to make the wrong decisions as the right ones, don't you think? And also, whatever fears you're feeling are more likely to get the best of you without a sense of mission to get you though challenging times.

## VIRGINIA:

Having a sense of mission in the way we've been talking about it has been tremendously important to me, and I'm absolutely certain it's helped me get through some really rough patches in my life; it's certainly helped me not give in to whatever fears I've been feeling. As we've talked about my time at Purdue and my Lighthouse experience, two things have gotten clearer to me about mission, at least as it's played out in my life. First, I don't think I've ever really consciously or deliberately tried to define my mission—not ever as far as I recall—as part of some kind of formal planning exercise. I'm not saying that I haven't given a lot of thought to my calling at one time or another, just that it seems to have come out of my experience, like a discovery, rather than some kind of plan. And the more I think about it, the clearer I see that my mission has evolved over time, hasn't been a static thing. In one of our interview sessions, we talked about customer service being my driving mission at Purdue; it's what made my experience there most meaningful to me. I got incredible satisfaction from helping my primary customers—the president and provost—succeed in their roles, and it felt great to expand my market to include vice presidents and deans.

But my mission has definitely changed since I've come to the Lighthouse. I didn't plan for it to be different in any formal way, I discovered it, this new mission, and, as I've said before, it's brought powerful new meaning to my life: helping blind and visually impaired kids and adults reach their full potential. I still have customers, but the barriers I'm helping them overcome—not only blindness, but related obstacles like low expectations and lack of access to essential technology—are so much greater than with my relatively privileged Purdue customers. I'm sure you'll remember the story I told about plucking the young fellow out of an office job and offering him a position as an assistant in the Lighthouse's music production program, because I recognized that his calling was as a musician, and I couldn't stand seeing him become the victim of low expectations. That's my newfound mission in a nutshell, and I love it!

What can I tell our readers about coming up with their own mission, their unique calling or reason for being? Well, I'm no expert in this kind of thing, I've only got my experience to draw on, but to me it's critical for you to pay attention and listen to what's going on inside you, to what you're feeling. If you're doing something you love, that really gets you revved up and energized, makes you feel passionate, then you're probably pretty close to your mission in life. But, you know, it's not just feelings of joy you've got to be on the lookout for; I like the idea we've discussed of Hillman's "daimon" speaking to us in negative or disruptive ways when we're keeping our mission at arm's length. As we've discussed, M. Scott Peck, in *The Road Less Traveled*, says that anxiety can be a symptom of mental health, because it's a voice from inside telling us that we're missing our calling. I'm getting the impression these days that many people, unfortunately, are just saying to themselves that anxiety is some kind of pain, so they're rushing out to find something to anesthetize themselves with, be it alcohol, medicine, whatever. One thing I'm really sure of is that if you're one of those high-achieving Type A's, like I suppose I am, you've got to be really careful that you don't just charge ahead with planning, setting specific goals, without listening. I've seen plenty of smart people plan themselves away from their mission. I think that's probably what the term "quiet desperation" describes.

## DOUG:

While you were talking just now, Virginia, I was thinking of my own experience about ignoring and then eventually understanding my own true calling, which we've discussed a couple of times. As you well know, I'm hardly a role model for creative, orderly change and growth in my life. It took me years of working in administrative jobs that I did well enough, but that didn't give me any deep satisfaction, and I began to medicate myself against the anxiety that just kept getting stronger. I certainly didn't listen to the daimon speaking for a long time, just kept feeling more depressed, until I realized that if I didn't make a dramatic break, I'd end up as a real alcoholic. So I resigned my last catch-the-train-every-morning job as a community college executive to go out on my own as a writer and consultant. That was twenty-five years ago, and I've gotten better, haltingly, at listening to the daimon as the years have passed, but it's a never-ending discovery process, at least for me. Without getting into all the gory details, I'll share with you that as recently as four or five years ago, finding myself feeling empty, emotionally speaking, I listened to my daimon closely enough to discover that my real mission was teaching, that what I was meant to do was teach by writing, speaking, and consulting, and this deeper understanding of my calling has enabled me to take my work in directions that provide much deeper satisfaction. But, believe me, the emptiness at first felt much more like an affliction than a precious signal, and I was sorely tempted to escape the feeling than respond creatively to it. It's a never-ending battle, isn't it?

## VIRGINIA:

Never-ending, absolutely! And before we go on to the next lesson we want to share, I'd like to say a word about the spiritual side of what we're calling mission or calling. I'm speaking only for myself, of course, but I really do believe that God means for us to find our calling in life, so to me, those daimons we've been talking about aren't so much imps of some kind, as they are angels—angels that speak to us from inside, not some kind of dramatic visitation from above. To me that's what the expression "God's will be done" means. It's not that we look for a divine plan that's been laid out for us, and all we need to do is discover the right path to travel, of course not. But it's listening, listening, listening to God's voice inside, which means being quiet enough to hear.

Attending Mass is one way I put myself in the position of listening, but, believe me, I'm not saying being Catholic or even Christian is the only way of hearing God's voice. It's just my way, and every reader has to search for her own path. Prayer is another way of being in touch that I've told you about. Speaking of prayer, there's one that I say a lot and that we used to open one of our Women of Vision luncheons. It's definitely not tied to any religion. It was so beautiful hearing an eight-year-old boy say it: "Angel of God, my guardian dear, to whom God's love commits me here. Everyday be at my side to enlighten, to guard, to rule and to guide." Of course, I can't be sure there're angels, but during the course of the day, it's kind of like I've got some cheerleader there helping me, saying, "Yeah, go for it. It's going to be okay." So it works for me. That's all I can say. It works for me. And I think it would be tough not to have that. But there are probably people who can do just fine without it.

## LESSON #4:  KEEP THINGS IN PERSPECTIVE.

### DOUG:

As I've gotten to know you and your story over the past nine months, I've concluded that your success at both Purdue and the Miami Light-house—in coping with and overcoming your vision loss, discovering a new mission, and building a new, more fulfilling career—has a lot to do with your ability to keep things in perspective. Sure, you're ambitious and hard driving, and you obviously enjoy being CEO of a major nonprofit in Miami and all the public attention that goes with that, but you seem to be pretty good at keeping your ego in check, in the sense of not overreacting to slights of one kind or another. You're not one to personalize things and get easily offended, so far as I can tell. That was certainly the case with the incident at the department store dining room, when they didn't want to seat you at lunch because your guide dog was with you. You didn't raise a ruckus, but instead turned what really was a slight into a teaching opportunity and example of very effective advocacy.

I've also learned as we've gotten to know each other better that, even though you're a really driven executive who—I know from emails and phone calls—works on the weekend, you're able to keep things in perspective. You seem, anyway, to be a person who enjoys life and has fun. Let's conclude this dialogue with your talking about the things that help you keep an even keel, no matter how hard you work or how daunting the challenges you take on.

## VIRGINIA:

A skill that's made a real difference to me over the years is not to be ruled by my ego, especially not to personalize things or hold grudges. To me, it's the future that matters, not the past, and you can't afford the negative emotion of nursing grievances or, worse, looking for revenge. Over and over again taking this positive approach has paid off. You reminded our readers of the department store dining room incident, and earlier in this book I've talked about other times I could've gotten huffy, like dealing with security people going through airport checkpoints. Keeping my ego in its place has paid off on many other occasions, and it's probably helped me age a little slower.

Let me tell you another story that's on-point. It was my first year as CEO, but I don't remember if I was still serving pro bono or was permanent. One of our volunteers said to a Board member, talking about my appointment, "Can you believe the inmates are now running the asylum?" referring to me as an inmate. I didn't hear this directly, but another Board member I trust repeated it to me, and a blind Board member who heard it was outraged and asked other Board members, "Can you believe what so-and-so said about Virginia?" At the time, I just chuckled to myself, it didn't seem worth getting angry about. Well, this particular volunteer who'd made the comment came to the Lighthouse to see me one day and said, "Virginia, I'm so upset with you that you can't take a joke. This whole thing is being stirred up with the Board." I responded, "I'm really sorry. What you said was pretty inappropriate, but I'm not the one who's been talking about this with Board members. However, it's not going to do you or me any good if we hang onto this, if we don't work together and try to have a collegial relationship. So, I'll make a deal with you. I'll forget what you said, and then you forget what some of my Board members said about you."

It seemed to me that the meeting went well; I wasn't sure, but I thought I'd turned him around, which felt good and worth the effort. I didn't really share that with anyone because, you know, you say negative stuff and it becomes like a snowball. So I just forgot about it, and I'm really able to forget about stuff where some other people might dwell on it and think about it. By the way, the ending was happy. I was so honored when the fellow who'd made the bad joke called me a couple of years later and said, "Virginia, I want to nominate you for an award." Then I knew it'd ended the way I wanted. You know what? It wouldn't have done any good for me to have gotten huffy and taken him on with, "How dare you say something bad about me!" Instead I kind of laughed it off, and we made the deal to forget the whole thing and move ahead. As I say, it's an approach that's worked well for me over the years.

Another thing, it really helps to keep your sense of humor, even when embarrassing things happen. One of the most embarrassing, which I've laughed about in the years since it happened, involved my first guide dog, Tracker. Okay, this is March 2005. I'm serving as the pro bono CEO, and remember, I was appointed in February and the next Board meeting's in March, so really it's only like maybe five or six weeks later. And I'm so proud. I'm going to be going to my first Board meeting as CEO, and I'm bringing with me the 2005 budget, which was the first time the Board had seen it, even though we were a couple of months into the fiscal year. An auspicious occasion if there ever was one! This was going to be such a great Board meeting. Well, that morning a woman who'd put the Lighthouse in her will for several million dollars called our development officer and said, "I'd really like to meet Virginia. Why don't you and she come over and have lunch with me?" So, knowing that she was a significant person well worth cultivating and being very well prepared for the Board meeting that evening, I said, "Great. Let's do it." And before it's time to leave for lunch, she calls back and says, "I'm really sorry, but the dining room here in my building doesn't permit dogs. At our condo, no dogs are allowed, so Virginia, you're going to need to leave your guide dog back at the office."

Well, I say to myself, "Do I get into all this ADA stuff, or do I just say, this is one time when you're going to leave Tracker in the office?" My decision: leave Tracker behind. So before leaving about 10:30, I take Tracker outside to do his thing on the grass, and I tell my assistant, "I'll be gone a couple of hours, and if Tracker whines or something, just take him out on the leash and tell him to get busy." However, a big rainstorm comes while I'm at lunch, and it turns out they don't take Tracker out since he hates going out in the rain. So I get back to the office and around four o'clock, now that the rain's finally ending, I take Tracker out on his leash to do his thing, and while I'm standing there someone comes outside to talk over something. Well, I'm distracted, so I can't really tell, did Tracker do his thing or didn't he? We'd been out there for ten minutes, so I assumed that he did. As you've probably guessed, I was wrong, but I didn't know.

So now it's time for the Board meeting, and I go upstairs, and we're standing around having refreshments before the meeting gets started, when one of my Board members says, "What's this water on the floor," and I'm totally oblivious since Tracker's never embarrassed me before. I'm wondering what got spilled when another Board member says, "Virginia, are you aware that your dog has just urinated all over the floor?" So my first Board meeting began with several Board members mopping up the floor with paper towels. You can either laugh or cry, and laughing's clearly better for your health.

I've probably gone on long enough, but there are a couple of other things I'd like to mention that have helped keep my life and career in balance and, I'm positive, make me more successful. For one thing, I really make a point of exercising, and I've pretty faithfully worked out since my days back in West Lafayette. Here in Miami, I go to the gym two or three times a week at six in the morning, so I'm in good enough shape to manage an eighty-pound guide dog, and to keep sharp during long days that often begin with a breakfast meeting and go through the evening. My husband, Bob, and I even ride a tandem bike when he's in Miami. Maintaining my balance and core strength is tremendously important, and I'm pretty sure it's still neglected in traditional rehab programs for blind and visually impaired people, unfortunately.

Of course, exercising can present you with some unusual challenges when you're blind. Let me tell you about a humorous thing that happened back in West Lafayette, where I typically ran at the indoor track at the Purdue field house with my guide dog, which worked beautifully. Imagine, Doug, running blindfolded, trusting your dog to lead you around the track; it'd be quite an accomplishment, right? So I really had this routine down, but you never know what might happen when you can't see what's going on around you. It wasn't unusual, by the way, to have people move to a different lane when Tracker and I would come running around on lane one. So, one morning when I got to the track in the field house, it seemed unusually noisy, and unbeknownst to me all of the various ROTC units were working in platoons doing duck walks—getting way down and walking in a squat. I'm starting my run when I hear the professor of military science calling to me on the megaphone to switch lanes. But I couldn't do that since my dog would've lost his reference point if we'd changed lanes.

So I very confidently called back, "Oh, no thank you, my dog is trained to shoreline on the left," and I took off in my customary lane. Now, what I didn't know is that twenty feet or so in front of me was an entire platoon of Army ROTC cadets. My dog is also trained to get to the head of the line, so all of a sudden as my dog is trying to get me to the head of the line while going to the outside of lane one, I end up on the back of a very strong, 250-pound Army ROTC student, and I'm still totally confused. Why was this person down so low? Why wasn't he standing up? Why didn't my dog walk around him? My dog and I get up, and we continue to run around the track, and it's not until I finish my workout that someone tells me what happened. I can't say that I won't have to deal with even stranger things when I'm in exercise mode in the future, but it's worth it, believe me.

One other thing I'd like to mention might sound a little farfetched, but it's a morale booster and helps me keep up my energy level, and that's being able to appreciate lovely things by touch, even though I can't see them any longer. For example, Bob's hobby is antique cars, which I can "see" through my hands. These classic cars are amazingly tactile. I can feel the beautiful hood ornaments from the thirties, and the incredible tail fins from the fifties. And I still appreciate fine crystal. As I was losing my vision, a blind lawyer told me he and he wife had a beautiful collection of fine crystal glassware, and my first reaction was to wonder why they didn't just use plastic that wouldn't break. But I've learned better. It's delightful to drink a nice glass of wine out of a fine crystal glass, and I love to touch beautiful pieces of hand-cut crystal, which is very tactile and doesn't require vision to enjoy.

# POSTSCRIPT 1

## DOUG ON MEETING AND
## GETTING TO KNOW VIRGINIA

### OUR FIRST MEETING AND MY TREPIDATION

Virginia Jacko and I first met face-to-face on September 14, 2006, although we had talked several times by phone over the prior month. When my taxi from the airport arrived at the Miami Lighthouse for the Blind and Visually Impaired at 8 a.m. that day, I was feeling uncharacteristically apprehensive. The purpose of my first visit to the Miami Lighthouse was to officially kick off a major project—we called it the "High-Impact Governing Initiative"—aimed at strengthening the governing role, functions, and structure of the Lighthouse Board of Directors. In a few minutes I would be meeting Virginia, who had been the Miami Lighthouse's first blind president and CEO since June 2005, after serving in an interim, pro bono capacity for the prior four months. Most consultants probably feel a slight tingle of danger at the prospect of working with a whole new cast of characters when beginning a new engagement, but I had an unaccustomed case of nerves when I got out of the cab that morning.

In retrospect, I realize my trepidation had to do with Virginia's being blind. Although I had briefly interacted with a handful of blind people in various consulting engagements over the years, I had never worked closely with a blind chief executive in my twenty-five years of nonprofit consulting. So on the taxi ride from the Miami Airport, I found myself worrying about small things that seem a bit silly in retrospect. Was the subject of her blindness off-limits, or would it be appropriate to ask her about the history of her losing her sight? If we walked down the corridor together during my visit, should I take her arm? During the buffet lunch that was being served in the conference room during my meeting with Virginia and her top executives, should I offer to fill Virginia's plate? Not knowing the rules of etiquette really bothered me, since unwittingly committing a faux pas is not my custom, and the last thing I wanted to do was offend my new CEO client.

So I announced myself at the front desk in the Lighthouse atrium that September morning in 2006, keenly anticipating my first in-person meeting with Virginia Jacko, but feeling unusually apprehensive as well. Informed that Virginia was on the phone and would be out to meet me in a few minutes, I began to stroll around the spacious reception area, looking at the photos of current and past Board chairs, reading the framed letter from Helen Keller, admiring the donated oil painting by a prominent and much-in-demand Miami artist, Romero Britto, and glancing into the large conference room where a class of some kind was being held. Probably ten minutes had passed when I was startled to hear, "Doug Eadie, it's great to meet you at last!" Turning around and seeing Virginia for the first time, I was taken aback. "She is blind, isn't she?" I thought to myself. "Of course she is, you idiot, there's her guide dog." But for a couple of seconds, seeing her radiant smile, her bright blue eyes looking directly at me, her outstretched hand, I wasn't sure. After I walked over and we shook hands, Virginia turned and led the way down the corridor to her office, her guide dog, Tracker, at her side, briefing me on the day's agenda as we walked, and after returning a couple of phone calls, she gave me a personal tour of the Lighthouse. Thus began a close professional association that has been enriched by our becoming friends and now includes our creative collaboration in coauthoring this book.

## WORKING TOGETHER AS CONSULTANT AND CLIENT

I had first become aware of the Miami Lighthouse for the Blind and Visually Impaired in August 2004, when I presented a half-day workshop on building effective Board-CEO partnerships in Ft. Lauderdale for the Broward Community Foundation. Among the people approaching me with questions after the workshop was a delegation from the Miami Lighthouse. Virginia, who was then actively volunteering at the Lighthouse and would soon join its Board of Directors that September, was not part of the group. Two years passed without my hearing a word from anyone at the Lighthouse, so I was pleasantly surprised to receive a call from a senior Lighthouse executive in mid-August, 2006. He explained that Virginia Jacko, who had been the Lighthouse president and CEO for a little over a year, and who, by the way, was totally blind, had been briefed about my Ft. Lauderdale workshop and was very interested in chatting with me about my possibly serving as a consultant to her and the Lighthouse Board. She was, he said, convinced that the Board's becoming a more effective governing body would pay off in terms not only of better decision making, but also a more solid Board-CEO working relationship. He went on to say that Virginia recognized that now, early in her tenure, was the right time to move on the governing front, when she was still in her honeymoon period as CEO and before any Board-CEO relationship issues had developed.

What became the Lighthouse High-Impact Governing Initiative was fleshed out over the course of several telephone conferences with Virginia that August and September of 2006. We agreed that it made sense for her Board Chair to appoint a Governance Task Force, consisting of several Board members and Virginia, which I would work closely with as Governance Counsel to the Initiative. Those long telephone planning sessions taught me some very important things about Virginia as a nonprofit CEO that not only augured well for this high-stakes project, but also whetted my appetite for our working together. First, and to me most important, was Virginia's expansive vision for the Lighthouse and her tremendous passion for the work it was doing in the Greater Miami community. Early in our first phone conversation, I was keenly aware that this would not be just another consulting engagement. I was accustomed to working with high-energy, ambitious executives, but the breadth of Virginia's vision for—and her emotional investment in—the Lighthouse set her apart. You could not doubt that she felt truly privileged and excited to be involved in work that made such a difference in so many lives, and you could not help but be inspired by her vision of the Lighthouse as a national center of excellence pioneering in research and innovative services going well beyond traditional vocational rehabilitation. So, I was naturally excited by the prospect of working with this visionary and passionate leader.

Another thing I learned during our telephone sessions was that Virginia was one of those rare CEOs who are both really attentive listeners and avid learners, and that she expected me to be an equally enthusiastic teacher. There were aspects of the governing business she had not mastered—after all she had been a CEO for less than two years—and she intended to take full advantage of the knowledge and experience that I had accumulated in a quarter century of working with hundreds of boards and CEOs. It was clear early in our working relationship that it would not be long before she became a really board-savvy CEO who knew the governing business inside out. What a refreshing contrast with many CEOs I had observed over the years, who had fallen in love with the sound of their own voices and couldn't be quiet long enough to learn much from those around them. And finally, I learned that Virginia did her homework; being the quintessential A+ student, she kept you on your toes. Because she was obviously well-acquainted with my governance philosophy and my consulting methodology and experience, she could drill down in her questioning. Never had I been grilled so thoroughly before signing on as consultant to this exciting new board development project.

## AN EXTRAORDINARY CEO WHO HAPPENS TO BE BLIND

The Lighthouse's High-Impact Governing Initiative has been an unqualified success, transforming the Board of Directors into a much stronger governing body and laying the foundation for a rock-solid Board-CEO partnership that can withstand the inevitable stresses and strains at the top of a large, complex nonprofit enterprise. Otherwise, it is not likely Virginia and I would have written this book together. With Virginia's strong support and enthusiastic participation, the Governance Task Force came up with a number of recommendations over the course of its four-month life, which have been fully implemented since the Board adopted them in January 2007. Among other things, the Board adopted a governing mission spelling out its key governing functions, put in place a structure of Board standing committees to carry out its detailed governing responsibilities, and instituted a more effective process for monitoring and evaluating CEO performance on an ongoing basis.

As Governance Counsel to the Task Force, I worked hand in hand with Virginia from beginning to end of the High-Impact Governing Initiative, and I had ample opportunity to observe her in action in dozens of intensive work sessions. Early-on, of course, I tended to see her as "Virginia Jacko, the blind CEO." Even in the early days, however, on more than one occasion I would find myself momentarily forgetting that she was blind. I vividly recall a one-on-one meeting with Virginia in the small conference room adjoining her office late one afternoon about a month into the project. Tired after a long day of meetings, I found myself thinking: "Doug, my good man, get a grip! No matter how exhausted you are, you don't want Virginia to see you looking so droopy that she'll begin to question your enthusiasm and commitment." Then noticing her guide dog, Tracker, lying at her feet, I chuckled to myself. Virginia might have sensed the fatigue in my voice—she was a keen listener, after all—but short of a downright miracle, she was not about to react to the expression on my face.

Later I learned that I was definitely not the exception to the rule among Virginia's sighted colleagues, and I have laughed with her about my occasional concern during our meetings about what she would "see" in my face. Never having spent significant time with a blind person before my collaboration with Virginia, I was not sure what to expect at the onset of our work together. In retrospect, I suppose I brought with me to the Lighthouse a preconceived image of a blind executive as: someone living in a more interior world, more passive than the normal executive, who would be somewhat aloof and disengaged in interaction with colleagues, and who would not be making eye contact with people at the table. Well, Virginia was the polar opposite! Sitting at the head of the table in meeting after meeting, she was a dynamic presence whose enthusiasm was infectious—a commanding leader without the least hint of passivity. Always meticulously prepared, she was clearly in command—asking probing questions, actively facilitating discussion, and neatly tying loose ends. And, what surprised me most early in our work together was that she, her head erect, invariably turned to colleagues when they spoke, looking them directly in the eye. So much for my preconceived image!

As the months passed, I began to perceive a different Virginia Jacko: the blind CEO I had first encountered was transformed in my eyes, becoming the extraordinary CEO who, by the way, happened to be blind. Virginia was clearly an outstanding nonprofit leader: visionary, creative, decisive, the master of such complex CEO functions as financial planning and management, strategic planning, external relations, and fund-raising. She inspired trust and commitment in her executive managers, and took the initiative in developing the governing capacity of—and building a rock-solid partnership with—the Lighthouse Board of Directors. She ventured out with her guide dog into the wider world of Greater Miami and the state of Florida, serving as a highly effective ambassador for the Lighthouse, cementing ties with important stakeholder organizations at the state and local level, and cultivating donors whose contributions helped the Lighthouse expand and diversify its programming and upgrade its facilities. Even if Virginia were not blind, her extraordinary accomplishments at the helm of the Miami Lighthouse for the Blind would deserve a prominent place in the literature of nonprofit leadership and management.

# POSTSCRIPT 2

## WELLSPRINGS

### INFLUENCING OUR WRITING

As we grappled with how to interpret Virginia's personal and professional odyssey, thinking through the key messages we wanted this book to convey to you and our other readers, we were especially inspired and informed by six very different writers whose work, in our opinion, offers powerful insights about human growth and change. Although this is not an academic work calling for a survey of the pertinent literature, we briefly describe six of these authors' books that were particularly influential in this Postscript. Of course, we have been influenced by several other authors, including many whose writing is more current, but these six deserve special mention here because of the tremendous impact of their thinking on our writing labors. And, by the way, we do consider their work timeless in almost every respect.

Interestingly, you will not find any of the six on the change management shelf in any bookstore or library, which, sad to say, is crowded with books that are preoccupied with manipulating people into going along with change strategies that have been fashioned for them by their superiors. Along with the family members, friends, and colleagues over the years who have helped to define who we are, these six writers are in a very real sense our collaborators in writing this book.

Dr. M. Scott Peck's *The Road Less Traveled* (New York: Simon and Schuster, 1978) is fundamentally a book about changing and growing psychologically and spiritually, which experience has taught us is at the heart of self-managed, creative change. The book's "tough love" message is summed up in its first sentence: "Life is difficult." To Scott Peck "it is in this whole process of meeting and solving problems that life has its meaning. Problems are the cutting edge that distinguishes between success and failure. Problems call forth our courage and our wisdom; indeed, they create our courage and our wisdom. It is only because of problems that we grow mentally and spiritually . . . It is through the pain of confronting and resolving problems that we learn." Seeing problems realistically and confronting them squarely is the key to successfully traveling the road of change and growth, and, to us, Peck is correct in identifying courage and discipline as absolutely essential tools for making that journey.

In *The Soul's Code* (New York: Grand Central Publishing, 1996), James Hillman deals with another critical aspect of human change and growth: your mission or calling in life, which Virginia and I see as the preeminent driver of creative change. Hillman sees this calling somewhat mystically as your "daimon"—your "uniqueness that asks to be lived and that is already present before it can be lived." It is a powerful force for creative change in your life if fully understood and coupled with action. Knowing who you are in terms of what you are meant to be—what you are meant to contribute in this life—is a huge step in the change journey. As Hillman points out, your calling "may be postponed, avoided, intermittently missed. It may also possess you completely. Whatever; eventually it will out. It makes its claim. The daimon does not go away."

In his dialogue with Bill Moyers in *The Power of Myth* (New York: Doubleday, 1988), Joseph Campbell, who was one of the world's preeminent students of mythology, describes pursuing your unique calling as a state of "bliss," which he says is a "kind of track that has been there all the while, waiting for you, and the life that you ought to be living is the one you are living." Virginia will tell you that her calling in life is being realized much more fully at the Miami Lighthouse for the Blind than it ever could have been at Purdue University, despite her success at Purdue and the intense satisfaction her work there provided. As Hillman would say, "her daimon has made its claim," helped along by a catastrophic event that Virginia would never in a million years have wished for, but that in retrospect was the cause proximate of her new, more fulfilling life. She has, in Campbell's words, found her "bliss."

You might recall that Dr. Viktor Frankl spent three years as a prisoner in Auschwitz and other Nazi death camps in World War II, losing his new young wife and his father, mother, and brother in the Holocaust. In *Man's Search for Meaning* (New York: Simon and Schuster, 1984), the first of the many books he wrote over the course of a distinguished career in medicine, Dr. Frankl defines each person's "meaning" in terms of taking action in particular circumstances, no matter how dire they might be. Frankl believes that there is always an opportunity to act in some fashion, and that such action gives a person's life meaning. "Man is *not* fully conditioned and determined but rather determines himself whether he gives in to conditions or stands up to them. In other words, man is ultimately self-determining. Man does not simply exist but always decides what his existence will be, what he will become in the next moment."

To Viktor Frankl, suffering is one of the paths to meaning, an opportunity to "bear witness to the uniquely human potential at its best, which is to transform a personal tragedy into a triumph, to turn one's predicament into a human achievement." This is what the distinguished novelist Reynolds Price writes about in his *A Whole New Life* (New York: The Penguin Group, 1995). Struggling for four years with an excruciatingly painful tumor inside his spinal cord, Price emerges from the horrible ordeal physically diminished but blessed with an even fuller life. "So *disaster* then, yes, for me for a while—great chunks of four years. *Catastrophe* surely, a literally upended life with all parts strewn . . . But if I were called on to value honestly my present life beside my past . . . I'd have to say that, despite an enjoyable fifty-year start, these recent years since full catastrophe have gone still better. They've brought more in and sent more out—more love and care, more knowledge and patience, more work in less time." Virginia and I see her odyssey as a search for meaning in Frankl's and Price's sense of actualizing potentialities under particular circumstances. To be sure, blindness restricted Virginia's freedom in various important ways, but under those circumstances, Virginia took resolute action to realize her calling, her tremendous leadership potential, in new ways in a new setting, the Miami Lighthouse for the Blind and Visually Impaired.

Finally, Allen Wheelis's powerful and elegant little book, *How People Change* (New York: Harper and Row, 1973), examines another facet of human change and growth: self-consciousness as an essential path to expanding freedom of action in a person's life. More specifically, what Wheelis adds to the mix is the critical role of consciousness in expanding the possibilities for action. His particular concern is bringing into the light of one's consciousness hidden emotions that might limit freedom of choice, without the chooser even being aware of the limiting emotions, thereby expanding your freedom to take action. He uses his own life to make the point dramatically in *How People Change*: a searing boyhood experience at the hands of a sadistic, harshly judgmental father that left him with such performance anxiety (fearing rejection and harsh judgment) that for years he turned down speaking engagements despite his highly successful career, and on many occasions found himself in the embrace of the paralyzing "steel fingers" even in casual social situations when put on the spot. Those steel fingers that left him unable to speak in public were loosened only when he brought into the light of his consciousness the debilitating fears resulting from that terrible experience.

Of course, creative change and growth ultimately depend on translating understanding and intent into concrete action, to the fullest extent feasible under the circumstances, and one thing these six writers who have left their imprint on our thinking and on this book share is a bias for action. Allen Wheelis puts it beautifully: "A farmer must know the fence which bounds his land but need not spend his life standing there, beating his fists on the rails; better he till his soil, think of what to grow, where to plant the fruit trees. However small the area of freedom, attention and devotion may expand it to occupy the whole of life." If Virginia's blindness can be thought of as a fence, Virginia not only wasted no time beating her fists on the rails, she actually expanded the boundaries, both personally and professionally.

# POSTSCRIPT 3

## THE MIAMI LIGHTHOUSE
## AT A GLANCE

Florida's oldest private social service agency for the blind, the Miami Lighthouse for the Blind and Visually Impaired, was originally known as the Florida Association of Workers for the Blind. It was established in 1931 with Helen Keller's encouragement and support from the Lions Club of Miami and the Miami Rotary Club. In the 1940s, the agency that became the Miami Lighthouse established a store and a number of sheltered workshops that trained clients in such skills as caning, rug weaving, brush making, sewing and basketry. In the 1950s, the chair of the Lighthouse Board of Directors, Dr. Bascom Palmer, requested that the Lighthouse assist in establishing an organization where he could do research and also treat indigent Miamians. In response, the Lighthouse provided seed funding for the creation of the Bascom Palmer Eye Institute at the University of Miami School of Medicine, which is widely considered the finest of its kind in the nation.

The 1970s saw dramatic change, as the name Miami Lighthouse for the Blind was officially adopted and the Lighthouse moved away from the sheltered workshop approach, becoming the first private,

nonprofit agency in the country to provide blind adults with vocational rehabilitation services. The Lighthouse was also accredited by
the National Accreditation Council for Agencies Serving People with
Blindness or Visual Impairment. The Lighthouse is currently guided
by an ambitious mission statement: "To provide vision rehabilitation
and eye health services that promote independence, to educate professionals, and to conduct research in related fields." With over fifty
employees currently, a $5 million budget, and a 37,000-square-foot
state-of-the-art facility in the heart of the city of Miami, only a quarter
mile or so from downtown, the Miami Lighthouse served more than
seven thousand program participants in 2008.

# ABOUT THE AUTHORS

**DOUG EADIE** is president & CEO of Doug Eadie & Company, a firm that specializes in building board and CEO leadership capacity and high-impact board-CEO partnerships. Doug is the author of seventeen other books, including two published by Governance Edge: *Meeting the Governing Challenge* and *Building a Rock-Solid Partnership With Your Board.* Before founding his consulting firm, Doug held several executive positions in the public/nonprofit sector, and he served as a Peace Corps Volunteer for three years in Addis Ababa, Ethiopia. Doug is a Phi Beta Kappa graduate of the University of Illinois and received his Master of Science degree from Case Western Reserve University. You can contact Doug at Doug@DougEadie.com and learn about Doug Eadie & Company at www.DougEadie.com.

Image by Cristian Lazzari

**VIRGINIA JACKO**, president & CEO of the Miami Lighthouse for the Blind and Visually Impaired, is one of only a handful of blind chief executive officers in the country. An eloquent and highly effective spokesperson for the blind and visually impaired, Virginia has worked closely with her Board in dramatically diversifying Lighthouse programming and more than doubling revenues. Virginia is a trustee of the Greater Miami Chamber of Commerce and of the American Printing House for the Blind. In 2007, Virginia was named Business Woman of the Year in the Nonprofit Leader category by the South Florida Business Journal. Virginia received her baccalaureate degree from Loyola University (Chicago) and her Master of Science degree from Purdue University. You can contact Virginia at: VJacko@MiamiLighthouse.org and learn about the Miami Lighthouse for the Blind and Visually Impaired at www.MiamiLighthouse.org.

## ABOUT GOVERNANCE EDGE

Governance Edge is a leading publisher of books, DVDs, and web-based programs on developing board and executive leadership, taking command of strategic change, and building fuller, more satisfying personal and professional lives. We are committed to providing the highest quality information available in the most appropriate format for our customers. Visit our web site, www.GovernanceEdge.com, for more information on our cutting-edge products.

LaVergne, TN USA
18 January 2010
170354LV00003B/2/P